love what
you do.

IGNITE YOUR PASSION. FIND YOUR
PURPOSE. LIVE LIFE WITH MEANING.

love what you do.

DANA SPINOLA

founder of fab'rik boutiques

Fedd Books
P.O. Box 341973
Austin, TX 78734
www.thefeddagency.com

Published in association with The Fedd Agency, Inc., a literary agency.

ISBN: 978-0-578-41281-8
eISBN: 978-1-5323-9229-0

Printed in the United States of America
First Edition 15 14 13 10 09 / 10 9 8 7 6 5 4 3 2

To my mom and dad,
thank you for teaching me how to dream
and how to work hard to make them come true.

And to my husband, Angelo,
for believing in my dreams—every single crazy one of them.

table of contents

"What you *do* is not your job title; it's the good work you put into this world."

introduction.

I slid into a bistro chair on the sunny patio of one of my favorite restaurants, the skirt of my linen maxi dress blowing gently in the light April breeze. Across from me sat Hayley, a friend of a friend of a friend in her late twenties who had boldly asked me out to lunch for career advice. I have a hard time saying no to bold asks, especially from women who have big dreams for their lives but are feeling stuck and un-inspired. I had agreed to hundreds of these types of coffees, lunches, and dinners over the years, but this one was a little different.

"Thank you so much for grabbing lunch with me," Hayley said. She flipped her perfectly highlighted chestnut hair over her shoulder. She looked gorgeous in her white blazer, jeans, and aviator sunglasses. I loved her style.

"Absolutely," I replied. "It's always nice to meet someone like you just getting started in her career."

We ordered and made small talk about our mutual connections. After the waiter dropped off our glasses of rosé and some bread, she took a deep breath and dove right in. "I really appreciate you taking the time to talk to me. I heard you on a podcast, and it was just so inspiring! Your story is incredible, and I know I can learn so much from you. Can you tell me why you started fab'rik?"

"Wow! Thank you. I hope the story lives up to your expectations." Then I began my typical spiel—company history, expanded mission statement, business small talk—I could probably recite it in my sleep I'd explained it all so many times. "I started fab'rik because I love fashion. Growing up, my mom made most of my clothes because we didn't have much money. I loved having a personal stylist, don't get me wrong, but I used to wish I could go into a high-end boutique and just buy a whole new outfit right off the rack. The whole idea of fab'rik was to create a boutique with that high-end customer experience but without the high price tags. That's why everything in our stores is under $100. I opened my first store in 2002 here in Atlanta. That store did well, and a few years later we opened another location and then another. It really wasn't the plan to have more than one boutique, but here we are now with over forty stores. It's amazing how God does that, right? Have you been in fab'rik?"

"Yes," she replied, her eyes shining. "I just love Stephanie at the Buckhead store. She helped me pick out these jeans and these earrings."

"I love that!" I replied. "You represent us so well."

"So I heard you have a nonprofit and that you're married with four kids and travel all over. What's that like?" Hayley asked.

I laughed. "You make it sound much more glamorous than it is, but yeah, right around the same time I opened my first store, I met my husband, Angelo. Since then we've gotten married and had three boys: Hudson, Lincoln, and Ryder. Then, a few years ago, we adopted our sweet little girl, Asher, from Ethiopia. And yes, free fab'rik is our nonprofit that hosts free shopping sprees for women escaping sex trafficking, and it's a pretty important part of my life."

"How do you have time to do all of that? I can barely keep up with my life, and it's just me and my puppy," she said.

"Well, I don't sleep that much," I laughed. "Although I'm getting better about that. I took a sabbatical to slow it all down a few months ago, and that really helped me prioritize how I spend my time. Now I go in later so I can take my kids to school, feed our chickens, and walk our dogs, Vader and Cowboy. And I block out time to pick my kids up, and we try to have lots of family dinners together. But I usually still sneak a little work in at night after the kids are in bed. I'm lucky, though, because I really love what I do, so it doesn't feel like work most of the time."

"I don't think I could ever handle all of that," Hayley said, shaking her head. I could see it in her eyes: dejection. She thought it was all so shiny and perfect and totally unattainable. Just talking about the highlight reel of my life wasn't going to cut it this time. So I decided to try something different with Hayley.

"So let me ask you: do you love what you're doing?" I said with a small smile, thinking back to another conversation, years ago, when someone had asked me almost that very same question.

"I like it. It's fine," she said. "I'm good at it. And I like the people I work with."

"Fine definitely isn't good enough. What do you do?" I asked.

"Well lots of stuff, really," she sighed. "I'm in charge of social media marketing for my company, working crazy long hours, but it just feels like I'm doing the same thing every day, and I'm not even sure if anyone notices. If it even means anything. I just want it all to mean something, you know?"

That's when it hit me.

Everyone asks, "What do you do?" Haley asked me, and I asked Haley right back. It's everyone's favorite conversation starter, right? But it's also so much bigger than that. That's when I realized I had been asking and answering the wrong question. For years, at every coffee and lunch and dinner where other women just like Hayley asked me how I started fab'rik, how I grew my company, and how I got where I am today, I would tell them about all the little pieces—the step-by-step how-to guide checklist for becoming a CEO and achieving your "dreams"—but I needed to tell them about the *big* picture. What I told Haley, and what I'm telling you now, is that what you *do* is not your job title; it's the good work you put into this world. Doing what you love isn't about having an enviable career or an Instagram-worthy marriage, house, or family. Doing what you love is about dreaming and creating a life infused with *meaning*. Meaning comes when you stop thinking about what *you* want and start serving others' needs. It's about finding the purpose that God has tucked away inside of you and using it as the rocket fuel that propels how you live, grow, create, and serve others. I don't think it's something you have to search the world to find; I think it's already inside of each and every one of us.

Well the *big picture* is that I started with love. I wanted to turn my shopping addiction into a career because fashion made my heart beat fast like a kid's on Christmas morning. It was my passion, and I loved everything about it. The corporate career I had been building at a big company just wasn't my dream job, and fab'rik was born when I admitted that to myself and decided to build a life where I actually *loved* what I did every day. But it took some time to realize that passion was only the beginning. My heart was beating, but the blood wasn't flowing. I loved the day-to-day, but the meaning wasn't there. I was living with only half of my heart before I found my purpose.

It took me a few years to find that purpose, but I've

been chasing it relentlessly ever since. I firmly believe that I was made to help women who have lost hope learn how to dream again—to remind them they are strong, beautiful, and more valuable than they could ever imagine. That is my purpose—my way of pouring love back into the world. My purpose was woven into fab'rik's purpose, and we made "High Style with Heart" our mission statement. We're whole-heartedly dedicated to making all women feel beautiful inside and out. To that end, we started free fab'rik, our non-profit that hosts free shopping sprees for young women escaping sex trafficking. We also design a clothing line called Asher (named after my daughter). Proceeds from the sale of the Asher line go directly to care for orphaned babies in Africa to cover their food, clothing, medical expenses, and education until they find a forever home. We use clothing, our passion, to fuel all of that good work.

Now I get to live a life where my passion meets my purpose, and as a result, my heart and my impact both keep expanding. I want to share with you how to love what you do from the moment you jump out of bed until the moment you fall asleep each night. I want to help you find the things in this world that make your heart beat so fast that you feel like you can't contain your joy. I want you to find the things in this world that bring you to tears as you feel your heart breaking—the things that are calling out to you to make a difference. Ultimately, I want you to discover how you can build a life around the sweet spot where those two things intersect—a life rich with meaning. This book is about finding out what you love to do and how to use that to change the world, heal hearts, and live a life that inspires and ignites others in its wake. I want you to give yourself permission to dream bigger than you ever thought was possible. And I want you to walk away from a life that doesn't fit you and create one that does.

DO YOU LOVE WHAT YOU DO?

So are you doing what you love? Do you really *love* what you are doing? Not just your job, but your whole life? Does it make you happy and proud? Does it serve those around you? I know that's a pretty bold first question for a book, but I'm all about big and brave and bold. We've got to make this life matter. It's not selfish to do what we love with this one precious life; it's a responsibility. You owe it to yourself and to the world to bring everything you've got to make it a better place for everyone.

It's OK if you aren't doing what you love yet. It's OK if you're looking around at your life, completely baffled as to how you got here, and wondering, "Is there more to it than this? Is what I'm doing making a difference? Is this what I'm supposed to be doing?" I asked myself all of those same questions a few years ago, and the answers changed my life. We tend to make it so complicated, but it really all comes down to heart. What makes your heart beat faster with excitement? That's your passion. What breaks your heart? That's your purpose. If you want to love what you do, you have to marry those two things together and live in that space.

By the time we finished our lunch and coffee, Hayley was fired up about finding her passion and purpose. She's just starting out and taking baby steps, but they are steps in the right direction, and I can't wait to see what she does next. Since I can't have lunch or coffee with all of you (although I really wish I could!), I thought the next best thing would be to write my story in this book so that it might inspire you to seek out what you love and use that to serve our world. My life unfolded in such a beautiful way because God dreamed big things for me, created and equipped me to do those things, and gave me the heart to chase them. I love what I do, whole-heartedly and without reservation, so none of it feels like work.

It's time to disrupt your regularly scheduled life. Start asking questions about everything you've been told you should do, everything you've been told you shouldn't do, everything you love doing, and everything you don't. My goal for you as you read this book is that you can get some unaltered, focused, exhilarating clarity about how you are supposed to be spending your life, dream up the best way to do that, and run full force toward those dreams while defining your purpose along the way. Instead of waiting for it to all fall into place, complaining, or blaming your dissatisfaction on something or someone else, you've got to get bold and take steps in the direction of your dreams. That's something important you need to know from the start—you are the only one who can dream your dreams and do the work to make them happen.

Your journey won't look exactly like mine, but I know that you will find yourself living a life that you love if you cultivate the gifts that God has already given you. You've got to bring those to the surface and use them to make a big impact in the world. Do it alone, or convince your friends to do it with you, but pursue your purpose through this book, and life will light up brilliantly. I'm going to challenge you at the end of each chapter to be bold, ask questions, delve into your heart, and seek the wisdom of those who know and love you to figure out what your life can really be. You have to have the desire to live your passion and pursue your purpose. If you want to live a life where you get to do what you love every day, you need to get brave and bold and figure out what that is. Are you ready to find out? I am.

"If you love what you do,

you'll never work

another day in your life."

ONE

what do you do?

I pulled my long, blond hair up in a bun and secured it with a pen as I balanced my purse on top of my suitcase and tried not to spill my chai tea latte. I sifted through the copies of *Vogue* and *The New York Times*, the process documents, and several bags of peanuts from the plane, searching for some quarters. Other travelers pushed past, jostling me as I finally found a quarter and slipped it into the slot on the pay phone. I dialed a number I knew by heart. A scratchy voice filled the air as a flight attendant announced a flight change over the loudspeaker. It was so loud that I almost missed that quiet, comforting voice on the other end of the phone.

"Hey, Dad," I replied, smiling despite my exhaustion. I was expecting my mom to answer, since Dad never picked up the home phone, but it was such an unexpected gift to get to talk to him. I'd been feeling stretched thin, but I knew talking to my dad would calm me down. He's a great listener and just has this knack for seeing right through to the heart of me.

"Hey sweetie," he said, and I could hear the grin in his voice. "How's San Francisco?"

"Well, it's California—it's amazing," I said, even though I never really saw the city while I was working fifteen-hour days. "Work's been really good. I got promoted to manager for this new project in my first week. It's pretty crazy, but I'm totally up for the challenge. I got to meet with the VPs, and we're redesigning their entire financial system," I bragged to my daddy, falling back into my best cheerful "fake-it-'til-you-make" it voice without even realizing it. I worked as a management consultant for Deloitte. My job was to go into companies, meet with their upper leadership teams, and help them figure out how to run their companies more efficiently. I spent most of my time jetting between Atlanta, Chicago, and San Francisco. I hadn't seen my parents in a few weeks, and I was a little (OK, a lot!) homesick.

"Sounds like you're busy," my dad said. "But how are you doing?" Clearly, he was not buying my "it's all good" act.

"I'm fine, Dad, just a little tired. Ready to get home to my own bed," I replied, looking down at my boring navy pencil skirt and wishing I could swap it out for something a little more "me." "I've got a to-do list about a mile long to tackle on the red-eye home."

"Dana," my dad coaxed, "That's not what I meant. How are you?"

"Dad, really I'm good," I said, adding a little more strength to my voice. "I'm completing all of my projects on time and budget and meeting some incredibly smart mentors. The partner on my last project gave me the top possible rating in my review. He said I'm outperforming all of my goals and that they could see me being a partner. I bet I could be one of the youngest partners at Deloitte if I keep this up. I've been meeting with some of the female partners to see if maybe one of them could be a good mentor."

"How's that going?"

"OK . . ." I said. "They are all super smart and encouraging . . ."

"But?"

I sighed. There was no use hiding anything from my dad. He would coax it out of me eventually. I could tell him now and get it off my chest or tell him later and get a big "I told you so!" on the side. "But they travel all the time, and it seems like a real challenge to juggle marriage and kids and these insanely long work hours."

"Well, do they seem happy?"

"Yeah. They're really all in on their careers." I sighed. I hadn't talked about this to anyone yet, and admitting my feelings out loud just made them more real. "But I want a husband and kids and to build a life like you and Mom did. What if I can't do this job and be the kind of wife and mom I want to be?"

"Oh, sweetie," my dad chuckled. "If anyone can figure it out, it's you. If you really want to."

"What do you mean, if I want to?" I replied. "I absolutely want to. I just need to figure out how."

Dad took a deep breath. "Dana, your mom and I are so proud of you. And, yes, I believe you could figure out a way to make it work. Of course you could. But, Dana, are you happy? Do you really love what you're doing?" I could hear the sad smile in his voice and almost see his eyes crinkling at the corners like they always do when he's concerned.

"Dad, you know I love my job." I rolled my eyes. "And I make a lot of money. I could be a partner, and you wouldn't believe how much money they make. Like crazy money."

If my dad could be summed up in one phrase, it would be this: *If you love what you do, you'll never work another day in your life.* It has been our family culture as long as I can remember, and I'd heard that phrase so many times over the years that it had almost become white noise. Both of my parents lived that way. Being artists, they were all in on their passions, but they'd barely made any money doing it until recently. Growing up with very little had insured money was a big motivator for me. I wanted to love what I did, but I had always thought that earning a lot of money would make me happy.

"Sweetie, I didn't ask if you loved your job. I asked if you love what you're doing. There's a difference."

My dad usually handed the phone to my mom for the big stuff, but this time he wasn't backing down. It caught me off guard, and his question suddenly felt big and urgent.

"No." The answer slipped out like a sigh. An exhale of honesty that I didn't even realize was in me. "I mean, it's not my *dream job*." I covered my mouth almost immediately, nearly dousing my red suede pumps in lukewarm tea. I couldn't believe I'd just said that. I felt so ungrateful to be making more money than I thought was possible and still not be satisfied. Why couldn't I just be happy with what I had? Why couldn't I let the idea of a dream job go?

"That's what I thought," my dad said kindly. "Well, sweetie, it's about time you figured that out. I know mom and I talked about how great it would be for you to have a job where you didn't have to struggle financially like we did. But, Dana, I just want you to live a life built around what you're passionate about and wake up every morning knowing it's what you were meant to do."

I felt tears build in the corners of my eyes. I blinked rapidly to clear them away. I didn't want to end up with smeared mascara. "What do I do, Dad?" I whispered.

"Sweetheart, you know what I'm going to say. It's your life. You need to choose the path that's in your heart and do what you were made for—what you love," my dad replied. All I could feel in that moment was relief. It bubbled up from a place inside of me that I'd almost forgotten existed. A part of me that was fueled by joy and passion. The part of me that wasn't concerned about paychecks and benefits and 401(k)s and the word *should*. The part of me that I can only describe as heart. "Now you get to figure out what that is. We can talk about it more when you get home. We just want you to be happy."

"I know, Dad. I love you," I said and smiled. It felt like he'd given me the permission to follow my heart that I didn't even know I'd been waiting for. "I'll call you later. Love you."

I hung up the receiver, feeling somehow both heavier and lighter than I had a few minutes before. I mulled it over as I walked to my gate, the question "What do you love?" repeating over and over in my head against the staccato beat of my heels clicking against the linoleum airport floor. When I thought of a dream job, I always thought of fashion, but I just didn't even know how to start making that into an actual career.

Trying to jump into the fashion industry with a degree in management consulting and no experience wasn't going to be easy. But every night as I tried to fall asleep and my mind slowed down from the craziness of the day, that question would settle over me and I'd sit up in bed, grab my journal, and start scribbling down dreams of what I wanted my life to be like. The volume of the white noise of my dad's motto inched louder and louder every day. I couldn't ignore it anymore. I liked what I was doing, but settling for *like* isn't an option when you know *love* is out there.

A NEW DREAM

A few months later, I woke up on my twenty-seventh birthday, determined that this was the year I was going to figure it all out. I love birthdays—mine and everyone else's! I love how the world seems to slow down and honor you for simply existing. I love the phone calls from old friends, and I really, really love the cards people take the time to actually mail. For my birthday, I took the day off of work. I went on a long run, blaring "Close to Me" by The Cure, sat on my front porch and caught up on all of my favorite magazines with a big cup of coffee, cleaned out my closet, and went out window shopping in a happy haze.

Every time the phone rang, I pounced on it. First it was my mom and dad. Then my sister, Erin. My brother, Sean. Our family believes in the art of the phone call, and I knew they'd all try to be the first to call that morning. Next it was my best friend, Shelly, from second grade. Then my boss. It seemed like everyone I'd ever known had called to wish me a happy birthday. Well, everyone except my boyfriend, Matt.

Erin assured me he was probably just having a busy day and would call after work. I met Matt at Deloitte, and we did essentially the same job, so I knew how easy it was to get caught up in the whirlwind of meetings, conference calls, and client dinners. I thought about calling him, but who calls her boyfriend on her own birthday? As six o'clock rolled around, I figured he'd be calling any minute. I reminded myself to be patient. Plus, I didn't want to pick a fight. We'd been fighting a lot lately. Matt had moved to New York City, but I was planning to move up to join him once we were engaged, and I was sure that would fix things.

I checked my phone again. Flip. Click. I'd flipped it open and closed so many times that day, I'm surprised it hadn't broken in half. No missed calls. I peered out my front door. Maybe he hadn't called because he was flying in to surprise me! I could just see it. He'd show up with a bouquet of white peonies, his suit adorably rumpled from the flight. We'd toast with freshly iced champagne and then he'd drop down on one knee and pull a blue box from his pocket. Proposing on my birthday would be so incredibly romantic!

I took my time getting ready for my birthday dinner with my girlfriends. I tried on about twenty different outfits and changed my shoes what felt like two hundred times. As I straightened my hair and swept shimmery gold eyeshadow over my eyelids, I daydreamed about how I would say yes. I didn't usually wear much makeup, but I dug through my bathroom drawer to find some waterproof mascara—just in case! I had a few minutes before my friends were picking me up, so I decided to call Matt. I didn't want to spoil a surprise, but it was getting late.

I dialed his number and waited for him to answer with a big "Hey beautiful! I'm right outside your door. Happy Birthday!" It rang and rang and rang.

"Hello," he finally answered tersely.

"Hey, baby," I said cheerfully. "How's your day been? Whatcha doing?"

"Fine. Just busy," he replied. He sounded distracted. "I just got home, and I'm going to eat and go to bed. Can I call you tomorrow?" Was he trying to trick me? Make me think he'd forgotten it was my birthday? Maybe I just needed to drop a hint.

"Well I'm just sitting here about to go to my birthday dinner with my girlfriends . . ." I said, "and thought I'd call and see how you were."

"Oh yeah, right. Happy birthday," Matt said, sounding guilty. My heart dropped. He wasn't on an airplane or on his way to my apartment in a cab. He had forgotten my birthday, and he wasn't even apologizing. Something was wrong. My stomach twisted, and I began to feel sick. Our relationship had always been up and down, and we'd broken up and gotten back together more than a few times, but this felt different.

"Matt?" a female voice called in the background. Who was that? Was it the TV? The radio? A neighbor out in the hall? No, it was too close, too loud. She had to be in his apartment. She had to be right next to him.

"Who is that?" I asked. I don't know why I even asked. I knew then what was happening.

"Can I call you back?" he stammered.

I hung up the phone, jabbing the "End" button so hard that it hurt. Matt was cheating on me.

The phone dropped out of my shaking hands. This couldn't be happening.

I expected him to call me right back. To say he was sorry. To offer a viable explanation. But my phone didn't ring again that night. A million dreams I'd had of our future together shattered in that instant, along with my heart.

Worst birthday ever.

Thick, heavy tears fell on my pillow as I tried to sleep that night. My eyes were practically swollen shut, and my throat felt raw from sobbing. But I still couldn't sleep. This breakup had me questioning all of my dreams and plans. This wasn't what life was supposed to feel like. Everything had been going so well. I had an amazing family and the best group of girlfriends, and I was a rising star at work. I had a job that let me travel and sit at tables with executives of Fortune 500 companies. I loved the rush, I loved the challenge, I loved that they paid for my dry cleaning! Everyone told me how successful I was. I'd gotten the grades, landed the job, put in the hours, checked all the boxes. It was supposed to be time for the next step—the wedding, babies, happy family part. Instead I was taking a big fat left-hand turn away from where I thought I was going. Heartsick, exhausted, and angry, I knew I needed a new dream. That one was broken.

After a week of wallowing in self-pity, I decided I refused to be the sad girl who got dumped on her birthday and didn't do anything about it or the girl who settled for a fine career that wasn't her dream job. I wanted to be the girl who did big, bold, exciting things and lived life fearlessly and intentionally, on her own terms. My dad was right. I was going to do what I loved, no matter what. I was more determined than ever to create a life that I absolutely adored. I wasn't falling for everyone else's definition of success anymore. I was tired of defining my worth by my bank account. I was tired of waiting on a guy to start living. I was tired of following rules that didn't make sense for me. And I was tired of leaving my dream life in the hands of others. When I thought about what was really important the answer wasn't money. It was passion. I wanted shout-it-from-the-rooftops LOVE for what I did. I wanted a life infused with inspiration and true meaning.

A BLANK PAGE

I needed to start with a blank page and take an audit of my life. I needed to really understand what I loved and what I didn't—where I stood and where I wanted to go. If I was serious about making those big, bold changes to my life, I couldn't dye my hair or buy new shoes and assume I'd feel different because I looked different. I needed to strip everything down to the bare minimum and then carefully and intentionally build it back up. I needed to curate my life the same way I would curate my closet. And, no, that does not mean I turned in my two-week-notice that day. I would never suggest you do that, either, because

I'm sure you have bills to pay! You don't have to go back to school or take on massive amounts of debt or do an *Eat, Pray, Love* tour of Italy to find yourself, and neither did I. I could figure it out in my regular day-to-day, because myself was right there. She wasn't gone—she was just a little lost.

I took the time to get back to the core of who I *truly* am and what makes me feel alive and excited. I needed to figure out what would propel me out of bed each morning and drive all thoughts of my ex out of my head, so I dove into my own personal happiness project. I made lists of everything I could think of that made me happy and unhappy. I revisited the things I'd loved doing as a child. After all, as kids we love without reservations, doubts, or restrictions. We don't know yet that society feels we're not supposed to love certain things or that certain ventures cost an enormous amount of money to get off the ground. We love what makes us feel alive and challenged—what makes our hearts beat faster. That's passion. And what we're passionate about is at the core of who we are.

When you were little, what did you want to be when you grew up? A model? An astronaut? A veterinarian? Maybe you wanted to write books or have babies or be an opera singer. When I was asked in kindergarten what I wanted to be when I grew up, I wrote, "The best," and I absolutely meant it. Whatever I became, I planned to be the very best at it. Back then it felt like absolutely anything was possible and everything was achievable. There were no rules about what you could do someday or who you could become. And that's still true. I want you to go back and remember what it felt like to lie in the grass, look up at the sky, watch the clouds go by, and feel like your whole life was stretched out before you and the whole world was yours for the taking, because it still is.

That's what I did. I went home, had dinner with my parents, snuggled with my mom on the sofa, watched my dad paint, and tried to remember what it was like to be little. The more I thought about it, the more I kept going back to my twelve-year-old self alone in my bedroom, ripping out pages from fashion magazines. I spent all of my spare pocket money on fashion magazines—*Vogue, Elle, Bazaar*—and I kept them all. Once I had a stack of new pictures, I would take my time carefully selecting spots to tape each one up on my walls, my ceiling, and, of course, the entire inside of my closet. Eventually the cut-outs looked like wallpaper, and I'd go to sleep every night surrounded by inspiring women being bold and beautiful. My room was my happy place.

While we didn't have the money for me to tear up the mall with my friends, I always managed to win best dressed thanks to my mom and her sewing machine. I'd bring her pictures of outfits I liked, and then she and I would go to Hancock Fabrics on the weekends to go through patterns and pick fabric to recreate the designer pieces I loved. She'd sew and tailor until each piece fit me perfectly. My soul would light up when my mom was pinning fabric on me. I felt so beautiful and special, like I had a personal stylist. My smile practically lit up the room when she would turn me around to see myself in the mirror. My mom even made all of my rush dresses for college based on pictures I showed her, which turned out to be a big advantage. I stood out in my perfectly fitting couture creations from the pack of girls wearing the same few sundresses from the mall. And she sewed a small "Made by Anne" label into every outfit she made me—a tangible reminder that I was wearing her love.

And it wasn't just the clothes I loved. I really loved the entire experience of shopping. My mom and I used to go shopping and put our finds on layaway. We had so much fun trying everything on, coming out of the dressing room to show each other, and pushing each other to try on things we would probably never wear. Even during high school, I loved going into high-end designer stores like Neiman Marcus and Versace just to browse and feel fancy. The experience of shopping at those stores was so luxurious! I loved how they would offer me a glass of chilled water and sit me down on the tufted leather stools to show me the latest trends. The dressing rooms were stocked with styles they'd handpicked just for me, and I'd try them all on with shoes they'd pulled to match. Their attention to detail was impeccable, and it made me feel like the prettiest girl in the room—even though I never bought anything. I became somewhat of a champion shopper in my twenties. Browsing local boutiques was fun when I was in a new city for work, and I was always the one my friends called when they needed help finding the perfect outfit to wear on a date—even if we mostly ended up shopping in my closet. Almost every conversation I had with my girlfriends started with "What do I wear to . . ."

Basically, I'd been thinking and talking about fashion my whole life. I just didn't really realize it could actually be my career and my inspiration all at the same time. Now that I was really thinking about what I loved and what I was good at, it seemed so obvious! Fashion made my heart beat—it was my passion, clear and simple. I mean, I almost lost sleep waiting to see what Carrie Bradshaw would wear in the next episode of *Sex in the City,* and I'd stay up late after each episode figuring out how I could recreate her looks on my budget. I studied the awards show red carpets like it was my job. Fashion was absolutely at the core of who I was from when I was little to now, and every day in between. Once I acknowledged that, I felt like I'd found my own personal yellow brick road. I knew I was standing at the beginning of a great big technicolor adventure—complete with stiletto-heeled ruby slippers!

WHAT MAKES YOUR HEART BEAT?

Figuring out what you are really passionate about is a big part of figuring out who you are. It may seem daunting to declare your passion and give it that big ol' important title, but it's easier than you think. What do you fall asleep dreaming about and wake up excited about? What could you spend all day talking about? What work would you do for free? What makes your heart beat like a little kid's at Christmas? That's your passion!

Still not sure? Ask your friends. They know. Ask your mom. She knows. Go back to your childhood, and look at the things you loved the most. Make a bucket list, and put everything you can think of on it—even things that seem impossible. Write down the things you've always wanted to do but maybe felt were too big or too scary. List out all of the things that make you happy—the big stuff and the little stuff. You'll start to see patterns emerge, and your happy place will become pretty obvious. Your passion might be gardening or being an incredible mom, yoga instructor, or jewelry designer, or it may have something to do with animals, painting, writing, or vegan cooking. There is no one-size-fits-all plan for life. If there was, everyone would be doing the same thing. Give yourself permission to entertain your wildest thoughts, because that's where the magic is. Please don't dismiss something because you think you are too old or too far down another path. It's never too late to learn what fuels you and give it space to bloom in your life. This isn't the time or place to think about what is appropriate or what you *should* love. Just be honest with yourself about what you actually do love.

Let's agree that *should* is basically a dirty word. *Should* shuts down the process of figuring out who you are and what you can do. That word, when applied to yourself, makes you smaller, less bold, and less confident in who you are. *Should* will tell you that your passion isn't practical or that you can't build a life doing what you love. *Should* prioritizes the status quo over your big dreams. *Should* can make it really easy to do what I did: fall into a career or a relationship that comes so close and looks so perfect from the outside but doesn't satisfy who you are deep down inside. It's a lot like buying a knockoff handbag. When you first buy it, it looks like a real Chanel bag, right down to the quilting and interlocking Cs, and it will fool almost anyone. But after a few years, the fake starts to show its lack of quality. The stitching frays, the pleather scuffs, and the Cs become tarnished. But mostly, *you* know it isn't authentic. It just doesn't hold up when put through its paces. And neither will your career or relationship when it's not the real deal. So if you can figure out who you are now, you can save yourself so much time later, and we all know time is one of the most valuable resources we have.

You don't have to hit a stalled-out point in your career or get dumped on your birthday to realize that you aren't doing what you were meant to be doing in this life. Those moments were the catalysts for me, but yours will likely look different. No matter what it looks like, the feeling is the same. It's the O-M-G-how-did-I-get-stuck-here sinking sensation in your gut when you look around and realize you aren't even close to where you know in your heart you want to be. It's the guilt that keeps you in a so-so life because you already told everyone you were going to do something and you're too embarrassed to change course or you think you've already invested too much time (or money) to stop now.

If you have those feelings, I want you to start with a blank page, too. That means figuring out, accepting, knowing, and owning who you really are, what you are good at, and what you love to do. You are going to need all of those pieces to pull this off. How do you know who you are, though? Like *really* know? One good place to start is to call your mom, dad, sister, or best friend—whoever your person is. This is the person who loves you, knows you inside and out, and will shoot straight with you, even if it might not be what you want to hear. Ask them what you are the go-to person for, what your best qualities are, and what they think your dream job is. For extra credit, you can even ask them what your biggest weaknesses and blind spots are. Tell yourself beforehand to be completely open. Without this info you can't move forward, and most of it will be things you already know about yourself but may have forgotten or pushed aside. This information is so helpful to jumpstart your heart. I mean, who doesn't like a few compliments from the people you trust the most?

When I asked my mom those questions, she said, "Nothing can stop you. When you were younger, you were always so sure of what you were going to do and how you were going to do it, and nothing or no one could stand in your way." I cringed as she said it, because it made me sound so bossy. But she reminded me, and I want to remind you, that every personality trait can be used for bad or for good. Think of your strongest traits as your superpowers. It's up to you to use those powers for awesomeness and know when to reign them in. My superpowers are the ability to turn a no into a yes, to always get back up when I get knocked down, and to throw a dinner party for one hundred people in under an hour in a pinch. I have relentless endurance, and I never give up. What are your superpowers?

Each of those strengths were given to you for a reason. They are a gift, and they have a purpose. Who you are is not an accident. What you love to do is not an accident. What you are good at is not an accident. God created you for something amazing. He looked around at the entire world and everyone in it and decided that the world *needed* you. He wasn't just trying to fill an empty space with another person. He created you to do what you were made to do. Have you ever really thought about that? It's exciting, but I also think it means we have a responsibility to figure out what that something amazing is. If you don't embrace who you are, the world will miss out on the you that you were created specifically to be and all of the amazing things you were created to accomplish. What a loss that would be! I don't believe that my love of fashion is simply happenstance. I believe that it's an important part of who I am. Not everyone is born with the belief that clothing can change lives, but I was, and I've used that to propel me into a place that is so much more than a job. It's a life built around my love of clothing that not only fuels my own passion but also serves our world in such beautiful ways. I want that for you, too.

You only get one life to live—one chance to make your mark on this world and chase down the happiness and meaning you were made for. The people who do what they love with their lives are the bold ones. They're the ones who ignore how the world defines success, and they define it for themselves. They are unapologetic, and they pursue their passion and purpose with reckless abandon. I couldn't wait any longer to be one of those people, and I know you can't either!

WHAT DO YOU WANT TO DO?

One of the first questions people ask when they meet each other is this simple, yet huge, question: "What do you do?" I never really knew how to answer it. The real version is "I drive my kids around all day, stress about what to make for dinner, and sprint into my office to hopefully inspire an amazing crew of women to change the world." But the dinner party version is usually more like "I own clothing boutiques." I leave out the mom stuff, the wife stuff, the daughter/sister/ friend stuff, the wannabe gardener, obsessive book reader, philanthropist with a heart to end sex trafficking and find families for orphans stuff because it's too long and complicated to explain the reality. What you do is not where you work. It's who you are. It is so much more than a job title—it's how we spend our time and what we care about.

At his school orientation, my nine-year-old, Lincoln, answered for me when another mom asked me, "What do you do?" He piped up and proudly said, "She makes people feel beautiful." WOW! I loved how that answer felt. That was the dream answer to the question about what I do.

While there is a dinner party version and a raw, gritty reality version, there is also a dream version of what you do. Take a minute to define each version and remind yourself that, while you may give different answers to different people, the dream one is the one embedded in your heart and the one I'm challenging you to pursue. Take some time to think about what you do and what you want to do.

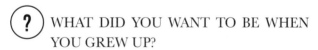 **WHAT DID YOU WANT TO BE WHEN YOU GREW UP?**

love what you do.

(?) WHAT DO YOU DO? *dinner party version:*

demand gen marketing at
a big tech company

(?) WHAT DO YOU DO? *reality version:*

Try to create leads for sales at
an e-Signature company

(?) WHAT DO YOU DO? *dream version:*

- Floralist
- Product designer (retail)
- interior design
- flip homes

"Who you are is not an accident. What you love to do is not an accident. What you are good at is not an accident. God created you for something amazing."

TWO

wise council.

I already told you that my family's mantra is, "If you love what you do, you'll never work another day in your life." Good advice, right? Of course, a lot of people might *say* it, but very few people actually *live* it. My parents always lived it. My dad, Myott, is now a successful business owner and no longer a starving artist, though most days you can still find him painting in his studio, blaring Genesis with a paintbrush in hand or playing air guitar in the zone. My mom, Anne, raised my younger brother and sister and me and then started her own interior design business. I love that I get to see her work in my favorite magazines these days. When I was growing up, she spent all of her free time making things beautiful. She could see the potential in just about anything. We would be driving, and she would pull over on the side of the road to pick up a sofa or chair someone had left out for trash pickup. "Can you see how beautiful this could be?" she'd ask. Somehow, she'd cram it into the car and take it home to be recovered. When she was finished with it, we could never believe it was the same piece of furniture. Even as young kids, we knew this was her gift.

My parents both started businesses fueled by what they loved down deep in their souls, so I guess I shouldn't be surprised that I eventually started my own—entrepreneurship and the desire to create are in my blood. My parents pursued their passions relentlessly, and they never made it look like work, even when times were tough, money was scarce, and a lot of other people would have taken the easier path. They had this intensity and peace funneled into what they did, and I wanted that.

Of course, to have the "love" part of our family's "love what you do" motto, you have to put the "do" part into action as well. And to take action, you'll need an idea of what you really want, so it's time to start dreaming. Dreamers tend to get a bad rap in our society, but dreaming isn't a waste of time—far from it! When done often and with purpose, dreaming is what keeps our lives on course. We're not talking about simply daydreaming—wasting time fantasizing about winning the lottery or having Channing Tatum showing up at your door to sweep you off of your feet. The type of dreaming I'm talking about is, essentially, intentionally imagining what your life could be. You have to believe in what's possible and be bold enough to put that out into the world.

When people talk about the best possible career for themselves, they always call it their "dream job." To find a job that's perfectly suited for you requires knowing yourself and what you are good at, what you love, and what you believe you can do. I knew fashion was it for me, so my next step was figuring out which direction I wanted to pursue. Fashion is a big industry with so many different paths. Did I want to be a photographer? A designer? A buyer? A visual merchandiser? I wrote down every job I'd ever heard of in fashion that sounded interesting to me. Some were real jobs, and others were just word jumbles like "trend spotting, shopping, styling" that I researched to see if those things lined up with actual positions. I read everything I could get my hands on about working with clothing. It helped me cross a lot of options off my list and get closer to the next phase of my life.

I did like some things about my current job. I really liked learning how businesses worked. I liked the behind the scenes of strategic planning and budgeting, and I liked the impact my projects had on the overall organization. I liked creating, planning, and beating goals. I liked going above and beyond to wow people. And I loved the idea that you got out as much as you put into it. I'd really taken that idea to heart, working seventy-hour weeks and climbing the corporate ladder so fast it's a wonder I didn't fall off. I was really proud of what I'd accomplished working full-throttle for someone else, but now I couldn't stop imagining what I could do if I put that same energy and intensity into growing something for myself.

In pursuit of my dream job, I stumbled on a career quiz. I dutifully circled my answers and then eagerly read the results. I had tied for two career options: magazine editor or boutique owner. I liked the sound of both of those, and they lined up with my dream job list, so I decided to pursue both.

I know now that the fashion magazine industry is notoriously difficult to break into—we've all seen The *Devil Wears Prada*, right? But at the time, I didn't really understand how competitive it is to land those sorts of jobs, especially in Atlanta. The fashion industry just isn't as big here as it is in New York or Los Angeles. In 2001, the Internet wasn't exactly the treasure trove of useful information that it is today, either. There weren't YouTube tutorials, online courses, or Buzz-feed quizzes. Most places still wanted you to mail in a job application and résumé—like actually mail paper copies in an envelope with a stamp. I didn't have any experience in writing, editing, or photography, but I was armed with the confidence that I could do anything I put my heart and soul into with enough hard work. Plus, I had years of great work experience, and I'd graduated top of my class from college. Why not go for it?

In typical Dana fashion, instead of mailing in a résumé, I decided to try to wow them and create my own mock magazine to send as my application for an editor job. I cut out images from other magazines, wrote my own articles, and then put it all together. I created a cover by cutting out headlines printed off of my computer and pasting them over an image. The table of contents was basically my résumé, telling them why I was the best person for the job. When I was finished, I sent my mocked-up magazine and my contact info to *Vogue*, my all-time favorite magazine.

They never called.

Is this a little embarrassing to share with you? Maybe a little! I'm sure that homemade mock-up probably got a good laugh in the Vogue offices if they even opened it, but I don't regret sending it. Going through the motions helped me try on that career a little bit. Turns out that I liked the idea of a glamorous magazine career more than I liked the actual work.

FULL STEAM AHEAD

At the same time, I started looking into how to open a clothing boutique. The idea of actually having my own boutique was so dreamy, it didn't feel like it would be work, which I guess should have been the first clue I was on the right track. Unlike *Vogue* (who obviously already had *Vogue* covered) there weren't too many boutiques in Atlanta, and there were none where I could afford to shop. The jobs at the top of my list were stylist, buyer, fashion merchandiser, and designer. Owning a boutique would let me do all of those things, plus I could open the shop in Atlanta and start putting down roots in my hometown. The more I thought about it, the more excited I became. But I knew that I needed to get some honest feedback before I invested any more time and energy into it. This was a big decision, and I wanted to make sure I looked before I leaped. So, I assembled my Wise Council.

My Wise Council is basically my inner circle. I always say it with capital letters in my mind because this circle of people is *that* important to me and how I work through life's biggest questions. God is the Chairman of my Board and by far the wisest Council member. He has assembled the most loyal and life-giving people to serve on my Council over the years. These people are my gut checkers, encouragers, and truth tellers, and they help keep me on the right track. They keep me moving forward and catch me when I start falling backward. These are the people I trust to be absolutely honest with me. They want what's best for me, not because it helps them in any way, but because they love me. And they aren't afraid to tell me no or redirect me if they think I've lost my way. I always check in with my Wise Council before making big decisions. None of us were meant to go through life alone, and having people who I know have my back helps me feel extra confident about my decisions. It also doesn't hurt to have them cheering me on and keeping me accountable.

I would encourage you to cultivate your own Wise Council. It might just be your mom and bestie right now, but don't worry—once you start looking for these types of people with intention, you will find them. Think about who you call when you are having marriage or parenting problems, faith or family questions. What about when you hit a career roadblock and need encouragement? Think about who you call to celebrate with you when you have good news, knowing they won't think you are bragging. Who is really smart, with opinions you respect the heck out of even if they're not what you want to hear? Who pushes you to be a better version of yourself? Who can you think of who wants good things for you, with no hidden agenda? Start with those people. My Wise Council at the time included my mom, sister, best friend, roommates, and a few work friends (my ex was obviously voted off at this point!).

I was pretty sure that opening a boutique might be my dream job, but I wanted my Wise Council's thoughts and opinions about it. It felt huge, and I wanted to know upfront if they thought I was crazy, before I took such a big leap of faith. So—dramatic as always!—I invited them over for a dinner party to announce my idea. I spent all afternoon making sushi and prepping cocktails.

After we ate, I gathered everyone in a circle in my living room and asked a big question. "After you hear about what I'm planning, will you please tell me if you think this is what I'm meant to do? Be honest— like really honest." They all agreed, and I started the presentation. "Imagine if I owned a boutique. Think exposed brick walls, concrete floors, and clothing that you'd be complimented on every time you wore it. Would you shop there? Do you think other people would?" To my surprise, they immediately got on board. "What about the name?" I asked next. "Envy, Pedestal, or fab'rik?" Everyone laughed at the name Pedestal (including me, what was I thinking?) but fab'rik, which is the phonetic spelling of fabric from the dictionary, they loved. All clothing starts as fabric, which makes fabric the core of fashion. I wanted my boutique to reflect the idea of getting back to the heart of things. Plus, my favorite memories as a kid were shopping for fabric with my mom, so the name felt very personal to me. I had expected at least a little pushback, but they all thought that opening a boutique felt like what I was meant to be doing.

With my Wise Council's blessing, I went full steam ahead. I was so lit up for this idea that it was pretty much all I thought about. I spent every evening and weekend researching the basics of owning a business, how a boutique works, how to create a business plan and secure a loan, and anything else I could think of. I grilled my dad for advice and read every book and article on entrepreneurship I could find. I reached out to any friend of a friend of a friend that worked in fashion or owned a business to ask them out for bold coffees, and I met with anyone who would sit down with me to talk shop, clothing, mistakes they'd made, accounting (*so* incredibly important!), and even how to actually ring up a customer. I was fearless in my pursuit of guidance, and I paid for more bold coffees during that time than I have at any other point in my career. I even wandered malls, just watching how it all worked. It was like drinking out of a fire hydrant of information, but I loved every conversation, meeting, and phone call. I was a woman obsessed. A lot of these coffees and calls were the start of lifelong friendships, and many of those same people serve on my Wise Council to this day. Once I had a good grasp on all of that very important, but not terribly exciting, stuff, I felt confident that this was what I wanted to do.

On August 1, 2001, I took the day off of work. I woke up early, feeling pumped—you know that morning feeling where you feel like you can conquer the world? I dressed like I was going to fashion week, opting for a killer pair of black pants with gold zippers on the side, a silky printed button down with a tie at the neck, and my lucky pair of sky-high black pumps. I carefully reviewed the sheaf of paperwork I'd neatly filled out before I headed out. Once I was sure there was nothing more I needed to do, I placed my stacks of paper into a white file folder. I had written "fab'rik" on one side of the folder and a big "xoxo" on the other.

I drove my battered, old five-speed downtown, singing along to TLC and dancing a little with excitement. I found a parking spot and marched into the big government building in front of me. I didn't have anything done for the business I was incorporating. I didn't have an address, an employee, or an actual piece of clothing, but none of that was going to stop me. I got in the long line to get a number to get in another line under the harsh, fluorescent lights, but not even the wait and dreary surroundings could dull my enthusiasm. While I waited, I realized that I was insanely overdressed, but I was about to be a boutique owner, so I had to dress the part. Finally, it was my turn. I handed over my incorporation paperwork and a check, and I answered some questions with a huge smile on my face. I was here taking a big, giant, scary step in my heels (of course!) to have a piece of paper that showed I was running toward my dream. It was the first item on my fab'rik to-do list, and it felt amazing to check it off.

Ten minutes later, I pushed open the door and walked out into the sunshine. I was officially a business owner. I immediately called my parents to tell them the good news.

"I think this is really happening," I gushed to my mom. "fab'rik is official!"

"Not surprised at all, sweetie. But I am so excited for you," my mom replied, and I really could hear the pride in her voice. "So what's the next step?"

"Creating a business plan that will wow a bank to get a loan, so I have money to actually build this store," I said. "I picked an opening date—one year from today."

"Isn't that awfully soon?" my mom asked.

"It actually feels like a lifetime away to me. I really wish I could do it tomorrow. But I think I can come up with a really good plan in a year," I replied with a shrug. "I could probably spend five years working on it to get it perfect, but I can't wait that long. The sooner fab'rik opens the better!"

THIS MIGHT SOUND CRAZY

If you look at the lives of most people you admire, you'll learn it took hours of dreaming and planning before they took that big leap of faith. I'd done the dreaming and the planning, but it all really came together thanks to a simple nineteen-dollar dress from Charlotte Russe.

After the incorporation files had been signed and approved, my roommates came home to find me holed up in my room. I was wearing my comfy white linen pants and a white tee, lounging against the big white pillows in my bed typing away on my laptop. My bed was a mess of papers, random notes, and discarded pens, and there was a huge assortment of business books scattered across the floor. I'd been working for hours without a single break, and I was tired.

The excitement of the morning had melted away as I tackled the business plan. There was still so much I didn't know. I was losing steam, and my mind kept wandering away from work and back toward my hurting heart. I missed the idea of Matt more than I actually missed him, but it still sucked. I knew I should take a break to eat and sleep, but I was worried that if I stopped to rest, I'd just start crying. Working on fab'rik was the world's greatest distraction, and I was genuinely more excited about my store than I had ever been about the idea of marrying Matt. I just missed having that person to dream this dream with, and it felt a little lonely.

"So," my roommate asked, plopping down on my bed. "Did you do it? Are you a boutique owner?"

"Yeah," I laughed, swiveling away from my computer to talk to her. "In theory."

"Dana! Why don't you sound more excited?" she pressed. "Ugh. Is this about Matt? He sucks."

I smiled despite that stupid feeling in my throat hinting I was about to cry again. "I don't know," I said. I felt like such a wimp. "I'm really excited about it. I just miss having someone to celebrate with, you know?"

She sat up and laughed. "Um . . . Dana. You totally have someone to celebrate with. Lots of someones. Me, for one, and all our friends, for the others. We're taking you out tonight so we can toast to fab'rik."

I shook my head. "It's not really real yet."

"It will be," she said. "So, we're going out whether you like it or not. It will be fun, I promise. We're all so proud of you." Then she marched out of my room, dialing her phone as she went. After a moment, she stuck her head back in the door, her phone up to her ear. "Hurry up and get dressed, we're leaving at seven."

I groaned. I knew she was serious, and I'd better be getting ready when she came back in, so I climbed down from my bed to get dressed. As I stood in front of my closet, I started to feel a little happy seep back into my soul. Looking through my rack of clothes, I realized I had an amazing dress I'd never worn. I'd been planning to wear it on my next trip to New York, but since that was off the table, I figured I might as well wear it tonight. It was a simple black, gold, and taupe patterned, Pucci-inspired slip dress with spaghetti straps. The fabric was silky soft, and I really liked the way I looked in it. Well, I wasn't saving it for New York anymore! I slipped it on and then checked myself out in my big mirror. And you know what? I actually felt pretty—a feeling that I hadn't felt in quite a while. The dress looked a lot more expensive than it's nineteen-dollar price tag, and I felt sexy in it. After finishing my look with fresh lip gloss, earrings, heels, and my favorite fringe clutch, I was ready to go. When I looked in the mirror again, I saw a strong, beautiful woman ready to take on the world. I felt like I could shake off some of the heartbreak and have fun again. One foot in front of the other.

My roommate and I met the rest of our friends for a fancy girls' dinner with really delicious bottles of red wine, and then we decided to go dancing at this little Buckhead bar called Metropolitan Pizza (now closed, RIP). We walked in like we owned the place. Usher was playing, and I headed to the bar with my roommate to order a cocktail before we hit the dance floor. As I waited for my drink, I spotted the most incredibly handsome guy I'd ever seen. He had warm, olive-toned skin, dark brown eyes with impossibly long eyelashes, wavy black hair, and a smile that gave me butterflies instantly. He was standing with a big group of guys in suits, laughing and having so much fun, and I couldn't stop watching his smile. I felt mesmerized. There was something so relaxed and calm about him. The last thing I wanted was a boyfriend right then, but something came over me, and I just knew that this was the man I was going to marry. That might sound a little crazy (because it is!), but I've never been more certain of anything in my life. I really think God gave me the gift of courage that night to make sure I didn't miss out on my soulmate.

I nudged my roommate. "See that guy over there? That's my future husband," I told her. I skirted the dance floor and made my way over to his table. "Excuse me" I said to his colleagues as I pushed past them to reach him.

"Hey. I'm Dana," I said and held my hand out to my dream guy. "I know this might sound crazy, but I'm going to marry you."

He shook my hand and smirked that Angelo-Spinola-I'm-up-for-anything-smirk that I now know so well. He responded gamely. "Maybe we should talk a little first if we're going to get married. Let me buy you a drink. I'm Angelo."

Later, he told me that he didn't think I was crazy. All he was thinking was, "Damn, I love how confident this girl is." The confidence that got me my dream guy was the same confidence I thought I'd lost until I put on that nineteen-dollar dress. We spent the rest of the evening talking. I told him all about my plans for fab'rik, and I asked him so many questions. I just couldn't wait to learn all about him! I'd never felt such an intense drive to know someone—and I mean *really* know them down to the core of their soul. Since we had already talked about marriage, I needed to make sure that Angelo was everything I hoped. The very first question I asked him was, "Are you passionate about your job?" No passion was a deal breaker for me. Watching my parents live out their passion for art and family together had given me sky-high expec-tations for marriage, and I wasn't about to settle for anything less. By the end of the night, my ex was a distant memory, and I couldn't wait to spend more time with Angelo.

Spoiler alert: Angelo and I were married a few years later.

That day I'd taken the first step to making my dream job real, and that night I took another bold step to meet my dream guy. The confidence I felt in that dress stayed with me, and as I built my plan for fab'rik, that feeling was my biggest motivation. I want-ed every woman to have the chance to find clothing that would make her feel as beautiful and confident as I did in that dress—no matter the size of her budget. That dress still hangs in my office to this day. It took a lot of blood, sweat, and tears to turn that concept into fab'rik, but that's where it started: with a bold little dreamer in a nineteen-dollar dress.

Had I not taken the time to really dig into what

made me happy, what I felt I needed to be doing, and what I loved, I wouldn't be standing where I am today. Yes, I'm thankful for the breakup that made me stop and ask myself those questions, but I'm also thankful for my Wise Council that guided me. (Angelo was obviously promptly added to my Wise Council.) Here's the deal: you don't get to live your ideal life accidentally. It takes work, and that work has to be done with intention to get where you really want to be. You just can't achieve what you want without knowing what you want. Then it's up to you to take the big steps and the leaps of faith to make it real. Sometimes you need to march downtown and complete a form to get the ball rolling, and sometimes you need to march over to a guy and tell him you're marrying him even if he might think you're crazy. There are no guarantees that either will work. But you need to be dreaming so you can spot those opportunities when they show up. You need to believe they are possible—like *really* possible. Who would have ever believed I'd start my dream company in the morning and meet the love of my life that night? Absolute best day ever!

WISE COUNCIL

Who are your people? Not the ones that agree with you about everything, but those people who tell you when you have something in your teeth, your joke wasn't really that funny, or you need Spanx with that dress? Who is the person you aren't afraid to brag to because they are your biggest cheerleader or the person you call crying because you know they will always take time to listen? Who inspires you, challenges you, and redirects you? Who tells you no when you need to hear it? It may be daily or once a year, but they pick up the phone, reply to the text, and would literally fly across the country for you. In my life, I call those people my Wise Council. They didn't sign up for the job—my heart assigned them. The safety I feel knowing they will be honest and that they have my best interest in mind, even over telling me what I want to hear, is what got them the job.

Think about people who know you inside and out and love you anyway, people who inspire you to do the right thing even when it's difficult, people you admire, people who you can tell God put in your path, and people whose opinions you respect. Make sure you have people from all of the different parts of your life covered (marriage, faith, family, work, and don't forget fun!). They don't have to be friends with each other—this isn't a group thing. These people will be your gut checkers, purpose finders, and honest truth tellers, and they will help keep you on the right path. I'll be having you check in with them throughout this journey, so take time to think about who they are. Since they know you, we are going to ask them what you are good at. You want to build a life not only around what you love, but what other people love about you.

NOMINATE YOUR COUNCIL

-
-
-
-
-
-
-
-

 WISE COUNCIL TEXT: I've been working on figuring out how to love what I do. I feel like you know me well, and I trust your opinion and advice. What are three things you think I'm good at?

 THINGS I'M GOOD AT

-
-
-
-
-
-
-
-

"Here's the deal: you don't get to live your ideal life accidentally. It takes work, and that work has to be done with intention to get where you really want to be."

THREE

wish lists.

I walked into the kitchen to find my mom sitting at the kitchen table working on her to-do list for the next day. I was fresh from a post-dinner shower with my pajamas on and my wet hair wrapped up in a fluffy towel. I'd been waiting for my mom to get my brother and sister to bed. Dad was working late, so it was the perfect time to talk to her.

"Hey, Mom," I said, perching on a stool next to her at the glass high-top kitchen table.

"Hey, sweetie." she looked up to smile at me and then went back to her little yellow-lined notepad. She made a few more notes, then glanced back up. "Everything OK?"

"Not really. I had a bad day at school."

"What happened, love bug?" she asked. She took

off her glasses and pushed her notepad to the side.

I squirmed in my chair, trying to figure out the best way to bring up what I needed to ask.

"Well I was changing for soccer, and my friends saw my "Made by Anne" label in the shorts you made me, and they asked me if we were poor since I didn't have real ones. I love all the clothes you make, and I know we can't afford Benetton sweaters, Guess jeans, or jellies like my friends," I explained carefully. "But are we poor?"

My mom smiled this confident, warm smile that only moms seem to have and said, "No, sweetie, we aren't poor. We're actually so rich in so many ways. We don't have a lot of money right now, but someday we will."

"OK." I nodded, but I couldn't shake that conversation that I'd had with my friends. At that moment, all I could think of was what we didn't have.

"Wait a minute. I know what we are going to do!" My mom jumped up got me my own lined notepad and pen out of her junk drawer. "Let's dream about what we'll buy someday when we do have the money."

"Come on, Mom, what's the point? Wishes never come true," I sighed. I could wish all day long for the money to buy all the cool stuff the other kids had, but a fairy godmother wasn't going to come swooping in to fill our bank accounts.

"Yes they do, baby," my mom said. She reached out and grabbed both of my shoulders, forcing me to look her straight in the eyes. "I promise you."

She seemed so serious and earnest. I guess it was exactly what I needed to hear, because I believed her. At first she was the one writing stuff down, but slowly, I let myself start dreaming with her.

"Where would we travel?" she asked.

"Ummm . . . Florida?" I wasn't sure what the rules were. What if I said the wrong thing?

"Italy!" she said, scribbling furiously. "Florence, Rome, and then we'll go ride a gondola in Venice!"

I nodded. That really did sound like a dream.

"What would we buy?" she asked.

"New cleats," I said, pointing to my old dirty ones by the door.

My mom laughed. "OK, so new cleats and all the other sports equipment you need. Now think of something fun—something frivolous."

"I know," I said after thinking for a minute. "I'd buy a fake Louis Vuitton bag."

My mom started to write my answer down and then stopped midletter. She looked up at me with wide eyes, "Dana Leigh, a fake Louis Vuitton? We are dreaming! It needs to be a real one!"

We both laughed. The best I could dream up was a fake designer bag? Suddenly I felt silly for limiting myself in my own imagination. A switch flipped inside me, and I realized that the sky's the limit and the only rule to this dreaming thing was that there were no rules. Dreams are really about having hope for good things to come in the future. Dreaming gives you hope when times are tough because you have a beautiful goal you are striving toward. My dreams got bigger and bigger from that point forward, and you can bet I never dreamed about a fake anything ever again!

DREAM SPACE

Do you know how to dream? Not the little ones, but the big I-can't-imagine-that-actually-happening kind of dreams? I didn't know how either until my mom taught me at our kitchen table when I was thirteen, and I haven't stopped since. Where is your version of my kitchen table? Find your dream space. It's not always a place—sometimes it's more of a state of mind. For me, every dreaming session is a two-part process. I wander and then I write. I usually start with a jog. Every time I lace up my running shoes and turn on my music, my stress disappears and is replaced by possibility. Then I go to my dream space to write. It's a little nook off of my bedroom with a distressed wood table and striped linen chairs I've had since my very first apartment. I run right there after my jog, throw down my earphones, and pick up my pen. I keep it stocked with some blank paper (I use a simple stack of printer paper) and lots of my favorite type of pen to make jotting my dreams down extra easy and straightforward.

Your version of wandering may be taking a hike or lying by the pool—the important thing is just doing something that opens your mind and lets you listen to your inner voice. Everyone's dream space will be different, too. It may be a quiet, cozy place like mine away from the world, but it may be that you think best amid the white noise of life. In fact, a friend of mine does her dreaming in bustling coffee shops.

Now, when you are stuck (and goodness knows those times will come), the best way to open the floodgates of your imagination is to create a wish list. Some people call it a bucket list, but wish list takes the death part out of it. Write all of your dreams down. If nothing comes to mind, remember what my mom told me: "There are no rules except that the sky's the limit." To get you started, there are some questions at the end of this chapter. You are going to have to get bold with putting some words on paper around the dreams in your head if you ever want them to become a reality.

Once I have my dreams on paper, I can organize them into categories. I use family, faith, fun, fab'rik, and friendships for my categories, but yours might look different. For me, dreaming is all big picture, wild ideas, and pie in the sky, but organizing helps me bring those ideas closer to earth so I can figure out how to take steps to make them real.

MAKE THE TIME

I start every year by devoting a whole day to dreaming. I try to go somewhere inspiring like the lake or a fun hotel outside of the city. But it can't just stop there. You've got to be intentional about dreaming new dreams and revisiting old ones often to keep yourself on track. I do this by building time in to my schedule for it regularly. The word "dream" is literally on my google calendar every month for a two-hour window, and it's something I almost never miss. I do exactly what I'm telling you to do. I start with a jog, then write down my thoughts. I always schedule these sessions when I won't be interrupted. I follow my "the sky's the limit" philosophy and don't put any rules around these ideas. Resist the urge to say, "I don't have time to do this" or "I don't even know if I'd be good at that." We don't have to be sure, we just have to be bold.

I have a few friends that would *never* put a dreaming session on their calendar. If I told these same friends, "Let's go grab a glass of wine and dream!" I'm pretty sure they would consider ditching me as a friend altogether. I get it—this may not be for everyone. So for those of you reading who can't imagine actually stopping long enough to pour life and inspiration into your future (wink!), will you at least buy a journal and throw it in your purse? This is one of the easiest ways to catch your dreams (yes, my kids call it my dream catcher). I keep a blank notebook in my purse at all times. I don't edit what I write, I don't judge myself, and I don't share it with anyone. (Except, of course, the time my purse got stolen with my journal in it. Now I wonder who out there thinks I'm crazy!) I use my journal to write down what my soul is feeling. Sometimes it makes sense, and sometimes it doesn't. Every few months I'll go back through them, looking for themes. So grab a journal that inspires you, throw it in your bag, and whenever you have five minutes, like waiting in the carpool line, at the doctor's office, or at the bar for your friends, pull it out and have a little uncensored dream session with yourself. I'd be lying if I said a cocktail doesn't add a little extra inspo!

It might feel a little selfish and self-indulgent at first to spend so much time thinking about yourself and your dreams, but I promise you it will benefit everyone around you. Employees want a boss who dreams big, kids want parents who dream big, and marriages need partners who dream big. When you are living your dream, you are infused with inspiration and happiness that seeps into the lives of those around you. It will become easier the more you do it, and even— dare I say—addicting! You will find yourself saying, "Imagine what could happen if we . . ." or "I think we could possibly try to . . ." You'll find yourself more inspired, more open to what could be possible, and one step closer to loving what you do.

GO ALL IN

You can't go all in on every single dream, so you need to focus in on one. Is there one that has been on the tip of your tongue, that you are so close to saying out loud? Or are you still wondering what it is? If you're still wondering, that's cool, but do not pass go, and do not collect two hundred dollars. Get back to your dream space, and keep working, but promise me you won't stay there too long. There is a big world out there that needs you to take what makes your heart beat and bring it onto center stage.

Aren't sure if your dream is ready for the big leagues? One of the best ways to start this process is to try your dream out. Can you test drive this idea without a big investment or declaration to the world? Who do you know that is already living this dream? Call them. Know a company doing something similar? Research them, visit them, and volunteer or intern there. In college, I thought I might want to be a pediatrician because I've always loved kids, so I volunteered at the hospital in Athens. Turns out sick kids don't like doctors. They would cry when I came into the room. It made me want to cry, and it helped me realize instantly that, while I loved kids, I was not made to be a pediatrician or any kind of doctor. It takes a very specific type of person, and that person wasn't me. (That being said, if you do this job, *thank you!*) I was very, very glad that I didn't wait until I was midrotation, post-medical school to figure that out. There's no risk to doing the work for free. If you don't like it, all you've lost is some time well spent. If you want to be a life coach, ask friends if you can coach them for free. Let them give you honest feedback. Going through the process will affirm your direction or send you in a different one altogether. Trying it before you buy helps make taking a big leap feel less scary.

OK, so maybe you can't quit your day job to go work for free (most of us can't), or you can't find somewhere to volunteer nearby. Let's approach this from a different angle. Look for someone who's already doing what you want to do, and see if you can spend some time with them. As you might have noticed, I call these types of meetings "bold coffees" because it takes guts to cold call someone you admire and ask them to meet you for coffee. Come prepared with specific questions, so you don't waste their time. Ask what they love and don't love about what they do, share your dream, and ask them for their top advice. Want to get super bold? Ask them to be your mentor. Take lots of good notes. Hearing from someone with their boots already on the ground should give you some great perspective as to whether or not this is the dream for you. My favorite question I love to ask is "If you were me, what is the most important first step you would recommend taking?"

Another way to tell if this dream is the one is to ask yourself, "What would I be willing to sacrifice for this?" Make no mistake, you will have to sacrifice somewhere to make a big dream come true. Something or several somethings are currently using up the time and energy you will need to follow this new path, so those somethings are going to have to go, at least for now. You will sacrifice sleep, free time, and potentially some relationships. While I was building fab'rik, I had to say no to girls' night and date nights more than I ever wanted to. I barely even managed to call my mom back most days. I was working around the clock, and I was so tired there were some days I would have traded every dollar I had for an hour-long nap. I basically lived off of coffee and prayer. I didn't sacrifice these things lightly, but I did sacrifice them willingly. I went all in because I believed sacrificing in the short term would pay off in the future, and it was one of the most exhilarating times of my life.

DREAM BIG

Of course, none of us is alone when it comes to dreaming big for our lives. My very first favorite bible verse was, "In their hearts humans plan their course, but the Lord establishes their steps" (Proverbs 16:9, NIV). I have big dreams, but I believe that God has even bigger dreams for me. He's the one in control, after all. I love that he inspires me to plan and dream, but ultimately, as the second half of the verse reminds me, God will handle the details and guide my steps as I walk with him through this precious life. I could never pull this off alone. I start my dreaming sessions with a pretty simple prayer: "God, please give me a curious mind to dream it and an open heart to believe it." We don't have to know how to get there; we just have to have the courage to put it out there.

It's a lot like when you are on your way somewhere new and you miss a turn and your GPS reroutes you. Where you were going doesn't change, but how you get there might. I try to hold tightly to the big-picture dream, but I hold the details to achieving it very loosely. As a result, I don't freak out if I miss a turn. I know my destination, so I can be excited about venturing down new roads to get there. At the end of the day, it doesn't matter which path I took to get there as long as I made it.

So dream! This isn't something you can skip or delegate. You have to do it for yourself. No one can do it for you, and even if they could, would you really want to live out someone else's dream for your life? No, of course not! It's your one wonderful life, so it's up to you to imagine all that it can be. Once you've dreamed all you can dream and you are certain this is the one, it's time to get to work turning your dream into your reality. That first step will be the hardest one to take. But once you take it, the next one will be easier, and the next will be easier yet. Soon you'll find yourself running full speed in the direction of your dream. Are you ready? Get your GPS out, lace up your running shoes, and let's go!

WISH LISTS

The truth is, we don't live forever. I know, I know—it's a morbid thought (and maybe I should have used the word bucket list), but come on, you know it's true. You only get one lifetime to explore, experience, create, and live. It's so easy to get bogged down in the day to day that you may never get around to achieving the fun, inspiring, meaningful stuff if you aren't intentional. I want you to think about the dreams you've put on the back burner and the ones you haven't really let yourself dream about seriously yet. Be selfish, be bold, and be honest. I want no rules, sky's the limit type answers. Dig deep, and no cliché answers (skydiving, swimming with sharks). I want the ones that are super personal to you.

A few things on mine are to take my daughter back to Ethiopia to see her orphanage; dance with my boys at their weddings; eat, pray, and drink with my sister along the Amalfi coast; have a fiftieth anniversary party where everyone is wearing white (my all-time favorite color!) at my parents' home and dance with my husband surrounded by one hundred grandchildren; create a girl's home in Africa; take down all of the outside walls of my house and replace them with huge floor-to-ceiling windows, regardless of the air conditioning cost, to let all the sunshine in; and to read the entire Bible.

So let's take a little time and dream. For some of you, this will be easy, but the rest of you may need a jumping off point. Imagine you had all the money in the world and unlimited time, and anything you did was guaranteed to be successful. Here are some questions to get you started.

(?) Where would you TRAVEL?

Bora Bora, Tahiti, Argentina, Thailand, France, Greece, Italy

(?) What would be your dream JOB?

Designing something. Florals, Interiors, Clothing products

(?) What is something extravagant you would BUY?

a vacation home in Europe - France or Italy

(?) What nonprofit would you START?

one to help girls become confident & comfy in skin. girls w/o families

(?) Who would you MEET?

(?) What would you ACCOMPLISH?

knowing that I created a career I love & family

(?) What would you EXPERIENCE?

Travel all over. make lasting memories w/ family

(?) What IMPACT would you leave in this world?

make a difference in other's lives - bring them to know Jesus.

(?) What else can you DREAM?

Traveling the world w/ my family

(💬) WISE COUNCIL TEXT: What do you think would be my dream job?

"It's so easy to get bogged down in the day to day that you may never get around to achieving the fun, inspiring, meaningful stuff if you aren't intentional."

FOUR

passion plan.

Dreaming, thankfully, is free, but the hustle to make those dreams come true—that's sold separately. There's no way around it, to love what you do, you have to *do something*. The year between filing my incorporation papers and the day I opened the doors to fab'rik was the most grueling of my life. There was just so much to learn and so much to do. But I was so passionate that it didn't feel like work. I was on a mission to make fab'rik a reality.

There are a lot of great success stories out there that talk about someone starting a company almost by accident—it was something they fell into or did on the side for a while. That is not my story. There is intention woven through every single thread of fab'rik— every hanger, every price tag, every pair of jeans, and every glass of champagne served. Nothing about that first store was accidental. I spent months and months crafting a business plan and fine tuning my concept. I knew I would need a loan to open up a store, so I couldn't leave anything to chance. I needed money for rent, utilities, lighting, a cash register, dressing rooms, clothing racks, and, of course, inventory. I knew in my gut that I had to get that business plan right or my dream would die before it ever got off the ground.

My Wise Council helped me figure out my blind spots and how to make my business plan better. They saw multiple versions, and I demanded that they rip each version to shreds and point out every flaw. (Don't I just sound like *so* much fun?) It was a little dramatic, but I wanted to hear the worst from the people who love me best so I could fix it before presenting in front of a bunch of intimidating bankers who didn't have a vested interest in me.

I continued to work at my consulting day job and also got a part-time job at another boutique on the weekends. They only paid minimum wage, but I didn't care about the money. I just wanted to see a boutique in action and feel the energy of starting dressing rooms, finding the perfect outfit for customers, and ringing people up. I was really trying the dream out to make sure it actually fit. How horrible would it have been to open fab'rik and only then learn that retail was definitely not my thing? Luckily, I loved it even more than I thought I would. The idea of getting dressed up for work like you are going to Fashion

Week was (and still is!) the world's best perk in my industry. I learned so much about customers from that little boutique. I soaked up every question they asked, every little thing that made them happy, how to market to them, what sales they liked, and what to do on slow Tuesdays to get customers back in the store. The more I learned in my research, the stronger my plan grew, until I was finally confident enough to set meetings with banks.

Remember that superpower I mentioned earlier? My relentless endurance? Well, I put it to the ultimate test during this funding phase. Week after week I would put my most conservative suit on and march into a different bank. I met with thirteen different banks, only to be dismissed thirteen different times. The first bank wouldn't even take a meeting with me. Ouch. All of that rejection hurt, but with each meeting I somehow fell more in love with my boutique and more determined to fight for it. I would have met with a hundred different bankers if I had to, but I'm really glad the number wasn't that high! Finally, my dad introduced me to a banker friend he played tennis with. I knew it was likely a courtesy meeting, but at the moment, it was my best and only shot. I had put so much into my plan, it was more than thirty pages, with the most beautiful photography and even prettier financial projections, if I do say so myself. I was so proud of it. I mean, there was a year of my life in that binder! I walked into this banker's office, and before we even sat down, I started barreling into my vision, mission, and financials. He reviewed my business plan and then told me that his bank didn't generally invest in boutiques, because they are considered high risk. He told me that if I wanted him to invest in me, I needed to show him why fab'rik would be different from any other boutique.

I went home and sat down and looked at my plans with fresh eyes. As I wracked my brain trying to figure out what would make my business stand out, my mind drifted back to that nineteen-dollar dress I'd been wearing when I met Angelo. I remembered putting outfits on layaway with my mom and dreaming about what I'd buy if I could afford it. Then I remembered the experience of the high-end customer service at Versace and being treated like a VIP. And it all finally clicked. What if I could create a place that offered the same luxurious customer experience without the designer price tags? fab'rik would be a place where you could spend under a hundred dollars, but you'd be treated like you were spending thousands every single time you walked in. You didn't have to have a million bucks to be treated like a million bucks. There it was, my first vision statement: to create a place where everyone could afford to feel beautiful.

It felt like I'd grabbed lightning in my fist. I was so excited that I had to hold myself back from sprinting to the bank to tell my banker my plan that night. I felt so confident in my belief that you shouldn't have to be rich to have a luxury shopping experience—I just couldn't believe I hadn't thought of it sooner! I made notes of every high-end experience I could think of, from walking the bag around the register and handing it to the customer face-to-face to bringing new arrivals to customers' homes for them to try on. At the time, luxury water was just becoming a thing, so I added a water bar to my plans. I'd have a bevy of designer water options to offer each customer in addition to wine and champagne. I planned to keep notes on each customer in a notebook that I called my Little Black Book—tracking the basics like sizes, favorite colors, and brands, but also kids' names, anniversaries, birthdays, and planned vacations. I decided to add an Xbox in the back so husbands would enjoy hanging out while their wives shopped. We would stock only a certain number of each item so my customers would be assured they wouldn't run into someone else with the same outfit at the same party. But my hill to die on was keeping my prices low. The window-shopping-only girl I'd once been would have adored fab'rik, and I wanted to stick to my belief that every woman deserved to feel beautiful, even on a limited budget.

Luckily, my banker caught the vision. I got a line of credit for $70,000, which might sound like a lot, but it wasn't that much when you think about all it had to cover. With my loan secured, my next big orders of business were to find my dream location and buy my inventory. Both were much easier said than done.

HUSTLE MODE

Have you ever given any thought to how clothing is selected for your favorite stores? I hadn't either! I originally planned to design all of the clothes for fab'rik myself and have them manufactured, but the more I researched it, the more I realized how unrealistic that was. I didn't have any design experience, and just planning the store was taking up every minute of free time I had. So my next stop was Americasmart, a maze of three multi-story towers where buyers came from all over the nation to purchase merchandise from manufacturers. It's such a large market that I hoped I'd be able to place all of my orders in one day and be ready to focus on other details. Yeah, that's not what happened at all.

It took me months to select my opening inventory. This market can easily overwhelm you with the amount of options to choose from. There are thousands of showrooms, and navigating your way can be daunting at first. If I found a dress or top that was the right look, it was inevitably way too expensive for my hundred-dollar-per-item cap, and if I could afford something, it just wasn't my style. I spent weeks scouring the Mart before I stumbled on the Hyman Showroom. Stepping into that showroom was a bright light of hope. I could feel the gray clouds parting and the distant whisper of a Hallelujah chorus. I say whisper because it was the first time I'd seen anything close to what I was looking for, but there wasn't enough there to fill my whole boutique. Still, I took that whisper and introduced myself to the showroom owner. I explained who I was and what I was trying to do. I shared that the Mart was so overwhelming and any direction she could give me would be a lifesaver. Unlike many other people who had been secretive and guarded about helping a newbie like me, Paula was an open book. She introduced me to other showrooms and, thanks to her, I left that day with a long list of contacts to help me finish building my initial inventory. That's when the real magic happened. I visited every showroom on Paula's list and called every name she gave me. I popped into every boutique I could find, looking for designers and lines that I liked enough to contact directly. I flew to New York and Los Angeles to find brands and styles that I wasn't already seeing in Atlanta. I was getting the hang of being a buyer, and I loved it.

I debated every single selection nearly to death. Did I have enough tees? Too many tees? Was this small, independent line from Los Angeles too Cali cool for Southern girls? Or was it exactly what we were missing? Were these earrings too trendy? A ninety-eight retail price would be over a hundred with tax—was this dress too expensive? Would I wear these edgy lace shorts? Would my friends? I would wake up in the middle of the night in a panic, mumbling about frayed-edge denim, and leave myself half-asleep notes that said nonsense like "asymmetrical boho dress" or "feather necklace." The day I ordered the last of my initial inventory, I was so relieved. But all of that obsessing did me a big favor. I spent a lot of time with each of my suppliers, asking questions, discussing options, and as a result, really getting to know them. Turns out we had a lot in common, including our love of fashion and hearts for making women feel beautiful. Today Paula and I sit on the board of the Americasmart together, pouring back into a place that helped launch our careers. Creating and cultivating those relationships has been so important along the way.

When I wasn't having nightmares about not having enough boho dresses, I was scouring real estate listings and driving all over Atlanta, checking out every space that had a "for lease" sign in the window. I had a very specific vision in mind. I wanted exposed brick walls, concrete floors, and tons of light—that New York City SoHo/Tribeca loft vibe. You see that aesthetic a lot in boutiques now, but there were almost no spaces like that in 2002 Atlanta. I finally found the perfect space in a rather industrial, "up and coming" area, which basically meant rent was cheap. My space had been a print shop before, and it had all the items on my design checklist including exposed brick, concrete floors, high ceilings, and the plate-glass windows. It also had little to no parking and no foot traffic nearby, and it was on a street known for bumper to bumper traffic that most sane people avoided. But, of course, I didn't realize just how big those negatives were then. I just knew that I loved the energy of that space. I signed a lease and then got to work turning it into my dream boutique.

I called in the whole family to help me build out fab'rik. My dad and brother created the dressing room structures with chrome rods as my mom sewed yards and yards of white canvas together to create the curtains. My dad also built floor-length mirrors for me, which saved me a small fortune. Big mirrors are pricey! My mom helped me stencil my fab'rik logo on the rough concrete floors with the same attention to detail she'd used for years sewing her "Made by Anne" label into my clothes. Angelo carted box after box of inventory from my garage into the store. My sister and I hand wrote price tags for every single piece of clothing. We even called in my cousins to help hang all the inventory. Because every dollar mattered, my parents offered me furniture from their home for the store. My seating area included the sofa I grew up with and chairs from the corner of my parents' bedroom. We made tables out of old doors. It was the ultimate family bonding. Every piece of the store had our hard work and love built into it. I ordered wooden hangers with my logo prominently displayed in black. I absolutely loved unpacking boxes of clothing, steaming them to perfection, and hanging each item up, making sure all the tags were tucked in and the logos on the hangers all faced the same way. There was nothing so satisfying at that point as glancing back at a finished rack filled with clothing I would have totally bought for myself. My water bar was stocked with bottled waters and endless bottles of champagne.

With each element coming together, I turned my attention to opening night. True to my word, I planned the opening for almost exactly one year after getting incorporated. I wanted that opening to be an Experience—with a capital E. I invited everyone I had ever met and plenty of people I hadn't. I grew up in Atlanta, went to the University of Georgia (Go Dawgs!), and had a large extended family, so I knew a lot of people to call in favors from. I roped my friends into being models, and we created a runway through the center of the store, complete with a DJ. I called my favorite restaurant, Cherry, and they gladly donated food for the party. I ordered champagne by the case and staffed the shop with my extended family for the night. My friends arrived early in the day, and I styled each of them to perfection. At the time, fab'rik sold men's clothes as well as women's, so Angelo and his friends served as my male models. Having him beside me that day kept me calm and filled me with extra inspiration to make it to the finish line, since he had been walking side by side with me through almost every step of my dream. By the time guests began to arrive, we were ready.

I don't think I could have imagined how many people would show up for me and my little boutique. Hundreds of people came to the opening. People were lined up out on the sidewalk, taking turns to come in and shop. We were selling everything, and they loved the inventory, thank God! The fashion show was the highlight of the whole event. I stepped up to the runway last, strutting down with Angelo by my side. It was such a surreal moment, looking around at the store I'd created out of nothing. It felt like something out of a movie. fab'rik had been nothing but words on paper for the last year, and now I could reach out and touch it. Seeing my parents so proud and all of my closest friends smiling as I reached the end of the runway was such a high. We danced, people shopped, and I thanked everyone for their support all night. I went home, giddy and exhausted, but just so satisfied. fab'rik was a reality, and it was everything I had hoped for and more.

Now, you didn't think that was the whole story, did you? I might have gone to sleep that night in a dreamy haze, but I woke up the next morning at the start of a nightmare.

GET BACK UP

I rolled over in my bed and yawned. I had planned to sleep in, but the early morning light filtering in through my windows told me I hadn't succeeded. I stretched and then snuggled back down under my fluffy, white duvet, ready to fall back asleep until I remembered that it was Sunday—fab'rik's first day! My urge to sleep was gone, and I threw the covers aside and jumped out of bed. It was 6:00 a.m. I raced through a shower and then slipped on jeans and my favorite black T-shirt with a silver layered necklace and snakeskin heels and ran out the door.

I couldn't stop smiling on the drive in thinking about my big opening night party. Life was so good! It was all downhill from here (or uphill or whichever one was the easy hill!). I was picturing how I'd answer the phone when customers called. Would it be a big sales day or, because it was Sunday, would it be slow? The only thing I knew for sure was that I was definitely going to need that venti soy latte I'd stopped for since I'd barely slept for a whole year.

But as I pulled up to the store my this-is-the-best-day-of my-life excitement was replaced with disbelief and a sick churning in my stomach as I tried to process what I saw. The side walkway was covered in glass, glittering like discarded confetti in the early morning light. The giant plate-glass window along the side drive had been shattered. The metal frame of the door was twisted and bent. I realized I was holding my breath and took in a few big gulps of air, trying to calm down. fab'rik had been broken into. I turned my radio off, listening intently. Could whoever had done this still be in there? I pulled out my cell phone and called the police.

I got out of my car cautiously and walked up to the store, my right hand clenched in a fist with my keys sticking out between my fingers. It was a pretty pathetic weapon, but it was all I had. Luckily, as I stepped through the gaping front door, it was clear no one was there. No one. And nothing. My store was basically empty. All of the clothes were gone, the register filled with cash from our opening night's sales had disappeared, the speakers had been ripped from the wall, and even the champagne in the water bar had been taken. All that was left was my parents' furniture and a few hangers on the ground. The concrete floor in front of me was splattered in blood, and my heels crunched more glass beneath them with every step I took. I closed my eyes, counted to ten, and prayed that this wasn't real. But when I opened my eyes again, I was still alone in my broken store. Did the people who did this not know how hard I'd worked to build this and how much I had poured my heart and soul into this place?

I think I was in shock. My thoughts were spinning and I was surprised to find that I wasn't crying. With shaking hands, I called my dad.

"Hey, Dana," he answered cheerfully. "You're up early."

"Dad, I can't believe what just happened," I whispered. "fab'rik was broken into. There's nothing left except broken glass."

"Oh, sweetie, I'm so sorry," my dad said calmly.

"Dad, what do I do? Who cleans stuff like this up?"

"I'm on my way now, I'll bring a broom. Welcome to owning your own business," my dad said.

I knew he was trying to cheer me up, and I grinned in spite of myself. "Thanks, Dad. See you soon."

Feeling a little better since I knew my dad was on his way, I looked around and took stock. There was a lot to clean up and even more to replace. I was going to have to do a lot of work to fix this. I didn't have a single employee, so all I could do was call and beg for help. My next call was to Angelo and then my landlord, Paul.

Within an hour, they all showed up. They brought brooms and dustpans and plywood to cover the windows and doors until new glass could be installed. They worked beside me all day to get the worst of the mess cleaned up. Needless to say, we did not open for business that day.

The police didn't make it over to the store until Monday. I was very confident that they could use the blood on the floor to catch the bad guys right away using DNA evidence. But apparently it doesn't work like that. Instead, they wrote up a report and told me to call my insurance company. So I did—that's why you have insurance, right?—only to be told that since the alarm didn't go off like it was supposed to, the break-in wasn't covered under my policy. Seriously? I was so frustrated and discouraged and angry. It felt like there was a rule book for all of this, and I didn't have it. Now here's the thing, y'all: I could have given up right then and there. I could have begged for my job back at Deloitte, paid that $70,000 back out of my salary, and gone right back to being corporate Dana. I mean, weren't all the signs saying I'd tried and I'd failed, so this was *not* my dream? Time to move on?

Nope. Remember my superpower? I don't stay down. It's like in those Terminator movies when everyone thinks the robot is finally dead, but just when they turn their backs, he gets back up again. Yes, I know it might be strange to compare myself to an evil robot, but I stand by it. I get knocked down a lot. I always get back up. I am so thankful for that superpower and that God made me full of grit, because sometimes that's all that gets me through—my stubborn refusal to give up. No way was I letting my dream die. No way was I lying down on that glass-covered, hand-stenciled concrete floor and letting fab'rik become a footnote in the story of my life.

First and foremost, I learned how to set my alarm correctly, and I never made that mistake again. Then I sat down and made a plan. I had enough left on my line of credit to replace the register and windows. But there was no way I could rebuy all of that inventory. And there was no point in reopening without clothes to sell. I got out my Rolodex (Yes, I'm old-school!) and called my vendors one by one. I asked them if they would possibly restock my inventory on net-30 credit. Net-30 credit means that I basically asked them to give me the inventory for free with the promise that I would pay them back in thirty days. It was a big risk for them since I was a completely unproven boutique owner, but I gave them my word I'd pay them back. It was all I had. I was so thankful that I'd taken the time to get to know my vendors and, in the process, had become someone these people were rooting for. Over half of them agreed to my plan. I was blown away. Half gave me a second chance. When fab'rik finally reopened, you can believe that I sold the heck out of that inventory. And thirty days later, I paid those vendors back in full and placed reorders on standard terms.

WOW

I never used to tell the story of the break-in, the breakdown, and the payback, but I do now because opening night didn't make me a business owner—it was staying the course through the tidal wave of trouble that did. Building fab'rik the first time was fun and exciting because I had so much momentum to push me forward. Building fab'rik the second time came completely from heart and grit. I was tired and discouraged, and giving up would have been easier, but it's only when things get rough and difficult that you really find out what you're made of and what you will and can do! I'm pretty proud of my little dreamer self that I didn't give up that Sunday morning. While I didn't know exactly what to do with my broken store, I knew it was my responsibility to fix it, and that it would be worth it. And it was. Dana Spinola, fearless fab'rik leader, was born that day.

Of course, that was just the beginning. To make my business successful, I had to actually make a profit. There's a reason most boutiques fail in the first year—it's difficult to find customers and then keep them coming back day after day, week after week, year after year. The location of my store left a lot to be desired in visibility and foot traffic, but I knew if I could just get women in the door, I could get them hooked. So I threw events and gave myself the reputation as the store that goes above and beyond. At first I was just inviting my friends and begging them to bring their second cousin, that girl that sat three cubicles down at work, their manicurist—basically anyone they'd ever met. Very slowly, I built up a base of customers that weren't people I already knew.

Because there was no social media, word of mouth was everything to me. I would host events with one goal: to have everyone who came talk about it to their friends the next day, which meant I needed to WOW them! From fashion shows with the Humane Society to blush-worthy striptease lessons and live bands, there was nothing I didn't try. I was willing to go the extra mile, pull all-nighters, and push the envelope to stand out over my competition. For Valentine's Day, I threw a huge party at the store and had everyone bring all of their single friends. I took a Polaroid photo of every single guest and wrote their phone numbers on the bottoms. Then I put the girls' pictures on the walls of the guys' bathroom and vice versa. It was like old-school Tinder, where people could look, see who they liked, and get their number. Two couples got married thanks to that event—you can bet those girls are lifetime fab'rik addicts! I threw a fashion show with the Falcons cheerleaders, who brought a few of the players to walk the runway with them. I went to all the nearby law firms and convinced them to throw their holiday parties at fab'rik, where I showed their employees all the new trends, made it easy for them to complete their holiday shopping, and gift-wrapped

all their purchases on the spot. I was the first store in Atlanta to offer customers the option to host VIP, private, after-hour shopping parties with their friends and take advantage of a special discount.

It was all about the experience, so first-class customer service was my top priority. I told customers they could call ahead if they needed something for a date or an event. They'd call me on their way home from work, and I'd get their purchases ready and then do a quick run up the street to Starbucks to pick up their favorite coffee. That way I could hand them their bag and a coffee to perk them up for their night out. I'd run bags and bags of clothing to customers' cars when they were stuck in that long line of traffic on West Peachtree Street in front of my store, sprint back into the store to run their credit cards, and then sprint right back out before the light changed. I sent personal, hand-written notes to almost every customer that first year, simply thanking them for shopping with me. I'd call customers to let them know I'd gotten in a new shipment of their favorite jeans, and I'd alert my size-five ladies to new stock of size-five shoes (because, let's be honest, size fivers, we all know how tough it is to find that size these days!). Before long, these girls were calling themselves fab'rik addicts, and, while we didn't have the most customers, we easily had the most loyal customers. It took me about a year to pay back my loan, and I hustled with everything I had to make that happen. Bottom line—I believed in my mission and knew it was up to me to take care of it, work hard for it, decide what made it different, and most importantly, not give up on it. What is that in your life? Are you chasing it, believing in it, and hustling for it with everything you've got?

I wasn't planning on opening more than one store, but my customers actually begged me to. Talk about supply and demand! So I opened my next store a little outside of the city. Of course, I couldn't actually be in two places at once. Not on my list of superpowers, unfortunately. So I started hiring teams, and that is when the almighty Ally Melson came into my life. She started as a stylist, but it didn't take long until she was basically running everything by my side. I loved creating new ideas, and she loved consistency. We were (and still are) a perfect match. I'll never forget when she first said, "Dana, I think we need a manual or something. I know you have it all in your head, but I think our team needs to be able to actually reference something on paper."

Most of the processes and procedures were easy to articulate, except for the WOW customer service piece that was so important to me. How do you train someone to WOW? It was almost like training someone to dream. You have to listen to a customer and be creative enough to figure out how to go above and beyond for them in a personal way. Did she mention that she loved fringe? Make a note in your Little Black Book and send her a fringe keychain for her birthday. Does she buy Fabulina jewelry every time she comes in? Have the designer custom make her a special piece for Mother's Day on us. I called this concept WOW, and I challenged each store to WOW as much as they could. One afternoon a customer came in and purchased a dress she planned to wear to an event that evening. We forgot to put it in her bag, and she was not happy. One of our stylists drove it and two other items from her hold rack to her house with a bottle of champagne and a note that said "Will you forgive us?" One of my most memorable WOWs was when we heard that one of our customers lost everything in a fire. Our team didn't hesitate to pack up bags of clothing and replace her wardrobe.

Whether it's a store owner, a manager, or a stylist, my team has made WOW a way of life. They look for little ways to WOW our customers every single day, and their thoughtful gestures make a big impact. While one of our regular customers was shopping, her babysitter cancelled. It was the night of a huge event she'd been looking forward to. Our team saved the day, and they not only offered to babysit, but they also did her makeup. One stylist even used her own money to Uber Eats food to a customer's family at home so she could take the time to find the perfect dress for her anniversary. Just like dreaming, there are really no rules to WOW, except that it should come straight from the heart.

After a while, we formally added WOW to our daily status e-mail so each store reported on it as a Key Performance Indicator (KPI), just like they would sales numbers. We prioritized it, rewarded it, and held it sacred. Eventually, going above and beyond for our customers became an integral part of fab'rik culture. Now I host a WOW Awards event every year at my home to recognize my teams that have WOWed me with how they have lifted our customers up beyond just selling clothing. WOW is the "Heart" part of our "High Style with Heart" mission statement in action. Other boutiques had sprung up selling high-style clothing with lower prices, but WOW is unique to us. We learned pretty early on that, while our customers loved our clothing, what they loved even more was how we made them feel.

Think about how you WOW, what is unique to you. You might not have customers to dazzle (yet!), but WOW isn't just about business. WOW is really a way of life. Remember those superpowers we talked about? WOW should be an extension of your personality, your strengths, and your gifts. It's taking what makes you unique and looking for ways to surprise and delight. For example, I love the power of a hand-written note, and I'm pretty good at remembering important dates and cheering people on. I keep a stack of notecards, envelopes, and stamps at my desk. In the morning when I'm planning out my day, I grab a notecard and write a quick note to someone I'm grateful for. It only takes me a few minutes, but it makes a big impact. I have another friend who is the best gift giver ever. She never forgets a birthday, and each gift is always so personal and thoughtful. She remembers throwaway comments and often gifts me something

I mentioned wanting or needing months before. My sister is the kind of person you can always count on. I'm pretty sure she has never missed my calls, and if there is something I can't do, she is always offering to handle it for me.

You might be the put-a-letter-in-the-mail type. You might be the friend who picks up kids from carpool or who always shows up with homemade cupcakes for someone's birthday. WOW shouldn't stress you out or feel like work. If you are feeling that way, that's not your thing. WOWs put positive vibes into the world and carry all of us on our bad days. Once you start WOWing, you'll be amazed at how it changes your relationships and the way you feel toward others. It will infuse your passion project with a piece of you and give it heart. You'll start noticing more details and find yourself looking for ways to WOW everyone. Use this for your plan. Can you WOW a potential mentor who took time to meet with you by sending them the journal that they complimented the day you met? Can you wow someone on your Wise Council who helped you through a big decision with coffee delivered to their door and a note that says, "Thanks for keeping me fueled!" Can you WOW the hiring manager for your dream job by sending in a resume that's a little more creative than a simple Word document? Maybe film a video of yourself articulating all of the reasons you're perfect for the job, or even mock up a magazine layout that outlines your best qualities. (Never mind, don't do that. I already tried the magazine thing and got less than stellar results!)

GET IT ON PAPER

Now it's time to WOW yourself by going above and beyond to launch your mission. Every dream needs a basic plan, even if you aren't opening a business. This is your Passion Plan. You don't need a formal, thirty-page business plan, but you do need to answer some basic questions to get yourself started. You want your mission to be crystal clear to you before you jump in. Remember, this is your passion, what makes your heart beat, what you love to do. So it's time to define the basics of the who, what, where, why, and how.

Why? Is it to make a lot of money? I started fab'rik because clothing makes me happy and I wanted to love what I did every day. It can be that simple.

Who? Who are you really doing this for? Me, myself, and I.

Why? At the beginning, I just loved clothes and wanted to do work that inspired me and brought happiness into my life. It wasn't until later that it grew to serve others.

As for the when? A goal is just a dream with a deadline. Set a date to take the next best step to move it forward. Write it on your calendar, circle it in red. Calculate how many days until that date, and let that number motivate the heck out of you. I write goal dates with a dry erase marker on my closet mirror so I see them every morning.

You'll end with how. This is where the record usually comes to a screeching halt, because it may involve money. My advice is to bootstrap it in the very beginning. Do as much as you can with as little as possible. It's difficult to get pumped about your passion plan when you have ten thousand dollars in debt hanging over your head. But if you want to actually start your own company, you will probably need a loan, and you will most definitely need a detailed business plan because banks like to see that you've thought through your overhead costs, operating costs, sales projections, marketing plans, and ways you'll grow and become profitable. There are so many resources with templates to help you lay this out online, and anyone who has done something similar can share the real-life lessons and wisdom they've gleaned on the job. I've found that most people are open books, and they are happy to help someone who is serious about accomplishing something.

Take a break, sleep on it, then come back with fresh eyes and an open heart, and look at your Passion Plan—really look at it critically. Would you invest in yourself? If someone else were presenting this to you, would you put your hard-earned money in their hands? Think through the pitfalls and the potential problems. Start solving them before they even exist. If this dream matters, make it a priority, and dedicate time to do it every week. No one else will prioritize it if you don't. Give this Passion Plan the best parts of your time, energy, and creativity. Complete the challenges in this book, walk through this process, and then make sure your passion still resonates.

After that, it's time for action. Make lists of steps you can take to make this dream a reality. Do your hardest thing first every day. Little by little, piece by piece, you'll be on your way to creating something amazing. Start small, and work your way up. The first step isn't always monumental, but it serves as the base you will build on. Once you've started, pick a date to do the big thing—start the podcast, find the space for the yoga studio, join the board. You can do this. Let's start the mission to love what you do. It's time to get it on paper!

PASSION PLAN

Time to craft a plan. What makes your heart beat? It can be anything! Jewelry design, photography, writing, or interior design—whatever lights you up inside. What did the little version of you want to be when you grew up? Maybe a teacher, nurse, chef, reporter, or life coach? All of these desires are linked to your passion, and they are deeply rooted in who you are and what you love. Your passion is not something you or others think you should be. It's what you love, no strings attached. It's what you would selfishly spend a free Saturday doing if you didn't have anything else you needed to do.

Time to declare your passion and create a plan to bring it alive in your life. Don't worry, this isn't too

complex—it's just the basics. You have to start somewhere, so take some time, and answer these questions
to bring your passion to life.

(**?**) WHAT: What is your passion? What do you
love? What makes your heart beat?

flowers, Traveling · design

(**?**) WHY: Why do you love this, and how does it
make you feel?

flowers make me happy & they're like
therapy. Traveling brings happiness & adventure

(**?**) HOW: What are some ways that you could
test-drive your passion? List any small or big
ways.

Help a Floralist for free. Take an AutoCAD
class

(**?**) WHEN: Pick a date to do something from
your HOW list to move in the direction of
your passion.

(💬) WISE COUNCIL TEXT: What would you
say my passion is?

"There's no way around it,

to love what you do, you

have to *do something*."

FIVE

pursue purpose.

I doubt anyone would be surprised that, at one point, I had so many clothes in my closet that the closet rod literally broke in half. I was hanging up one of my favorite dresses when the entire rack snapped and all of the clothing fell, pulling down the shelf of shoes above it as it crashed. There was clothing everywhere, and seeing it all in heaps on the floor, I realized I had way too much. I officially needed to purge.

I trudged down to my kitchen, pulled out some industrial garbage bags, and spent the rest of the afternoon sorting through each and every piece. I was shocked I'd let my wardrobe get so out of control. I knew better than this. I even taught my customers and friends my practically trademarked closet rules: If it makes you feel beautiful and you love it, keep it. If it is broken or needs to be altered, fix it. And if it doesn't fit or flatter, donate it. I started trying clothes on and sorting them into keep, fix, and donate piles. I didn't even make it halfway through my collection that day. It's actually kind of embarrassing to admit that I had that much clothing to go through, but I did. And a lot of it was barely worn or hadn't been worn in years. I bagged up so many sweaters (Why did I keep buying these? I live in Georgia—not Colorado!), suits leftover from my Deloitte days, and plenty of pieces simply past their best-by dates. I guess it's one of the hazards of the job when you own a fashion company. As the founder and face of fab'rik, I needed to look stylish and wear the most current trends. It was important that I show off our latest clothing while working in our stores, but even I could admit I'd gone a little over-board.

A few weeks later, I went over to my friend Kim's house for a glass of wine and girl talk. I respect the heck out of Kim, an anchor for the evening news, who is as driven and ambitious as I am. As we sat at her kitchen island, I told her about my busted closet. She admitted that she had just cleaned out her own closet and had filled her trunk to the top with garbage bags of clothes to donate, but hadn't gotten a chance to drop them off anywhere yet. First world problems, right? We were both embarrassed by our overcon-sumption and felt a sense of responsibility to donate these clothes the right way—whatever that was.

"I hate to just drop them at a charity shop or thrift

store," Kim said, scrunching up her nose and taking another sip of wine. "I want to know that my donations are going to someone who really needs them, you know? I'd like to donate somewhere where I could be more involved."

I stood up and paced around Kim's kitchen. I started to see an idea unfold in my mind. "Wait, imagine if we could actually go meet the girls who needed the clothing, give them the clothes ourselves, and spend some time with them. We could style them like we do with my customers at fab'rik, hear their stories, and remind them how beautiful they are. I have no idea how it would work, but I do know styling, and obviously you and I have way too many clothes." I laughed. "We would just need to figure out how to find these girls that need the clothing."

"Well that wouldn't be too difficult," she replied. "We've done stories on a lot of different organizations that help girls. I'm sure we could find some that would love to have us donate clothing."

"What if we could do free shopping sprees for these girls? What if we could get my customers to donate clothing and our friends to volunteer to help? We could take all of the clothing out of fab'rik and replace it with the donated clothing for a day, and the girls we're helping could experience boutique shopping without the pressure of price tags. Then we could invite these organizations to come shop at fab'rik for the day. We could help style them and get to know them and figure out what more we could do to help. Free sprees for those in need," I mused, my brain already working overtime.

"Absolutely. I'm totally on board." Kim nodded. I could tell she was getting excited. We both were!

"Since the day I opened fab'rik, I've wanted to do free shopping sprees. I never knew what that would look like, but I think this is it," I said, continuing to pace. "When can we do this?"

When can we do this? My younger self was even less patient than my current self! Within the week we had constructed a plan. Kim announced our plans on the news and encouraged organizations with needs to contact us. I sent out an e-mail to our fab'rik customer list asking them to bring any gently used clothing they wanted to donate to any of our fab'rik stores in Atlanta. Then we both sent e-mails to our friends and family asking if anyone wanted to volunteer. We were overwhelmed by the response. Within four days, our stockrooms were busting at the seams with donations, so we had to rent a nearby warehouse to hold over four hundred bags of clothing, with more coming in every day. We had a list a mile long of volunteers, which was good because we needed the help. We'd never done anything like this before, and we were figuring it out as we went. Over thirty different organizations reached out, including shelters, safe houses, and girls' empowerment organizations. Even families who couldn't afford back-to-school shopping in the wake of the economic downturn called and asked if they could attend the spree. We said yes to everyone.

When I created fab'rik I always said I wanted it to be a place where everyone could afford to feel beautiful. I knew I was taking liberty with the word "everyone" because there were so many women out there who couldn't afford even our low prices. This was closing the loop on that, as we were literally creating a free fab'rik. There was no feeling of burden in this new adventure—just peace. Yes, it was extra work and we would actually lose money by shutting down the store for a day, but it was crystal clear to me that this idea needed to be part of fab'rik's mission. The week of the event, we had endless volunteers working in shifts to organize the donations by size, get all the clothing hung up, and prep the shoes and accessories. We filled racks as soon as we set them up. We hung and steamed and belted and merchandised until our fingers were sore. We wanted the clothing to look like it would if it were hanging in a real boutique, to give these women the full fab'rik experience just without the price tags.

FREE SPREE

The Friday night before the big free spree, we huddled around our bright-eyed and bushy-tailed team of volunteers, including Ally and our entire fab'rik team. "Ok, y'all, tonight we are going to take every single item out of fab'rik—clothes, shoes, jewelry, and belts—and swap it with all of those donations in the warehouse next door so hundreds of women and girls can come shop here tomorrow for free. Are you on board?" I asked, hoping they wouldn't fail me now. There wasn't a single hesitation—they all just cheered and got started. One big group started packaging up the fab'rik clothing, and another group started bringing in the donations. The energy in the store that night was infectious, infused with a level of meaning that was brand new and so beautiful. We worked well past midnight and then came back bright and early a few hours later to find a line snaking around the block from the first organization we were working with.

That day went by in a blur. Each girl who entered was assigned a volunteer stylist who helped them select several full outfits. There were no rules that first Saturday, and to say it was chaotic doesn't even begin to describe it. It made my order-loving, introverted heart a little panicky to see my store crammed that full of people, with clothing flying everywhere. But it was also much easier than I'd expected because God was there, facilitating conversations and making sure everyone got what they needed. Kim and I had plotted this course, but man, was God directing the steps. The girl my mom was matched with didn't speak any English, but that didn't slow them down. Turns out fashion is a universal language. Girls hugged us, clutching Ikea bags packed full of clothing. Moms and organization leaders were thanking us with tears streaming down their faces. It was a powerful day that outshined every other moment I've had since opening fab'rik. We called the event "free fab'rik." We'd always been about high style with no sticker shock, but now we got to provide high style with no stickers at all. I loved it.

I got the opportunity to talk to a lot of the girls we helped, and I was blown away by their stories. There were so many courageous, strong, young girls stuck in such bad situations, mostly through no fault of their own. It seemed like they had given up on their dreams and even on the idea of dreaming at all. We made it a point to walk each of them over to the full-length mirror after we'd styled them so they could see their new looks. I think I heard, "Look how beautiful you are!" hundreds of times that day as I watched these girls break into the biggest smiles. Seeing how clothing can bring that type of happiness and confidence, if even for a day, was life changing for me. One girl told me she knew she could get all A's with her new school clothes. A mom told me she had been living in a shelter with her kids since she lost her job, and her girls had outgrown most of their clothes. With some new jeans and tees, they could focus on learning instead of keeping themselves covered. But the stories that struck me the most were from the women and girls who had escaped sex trafficking. Of course I knew it existed, but I had no idea that Atlanta led the country in sex trafficking. It didn't seem like that could possibly be true. Why wasn't more being done to put an end to that? It absolutely broke my heart to hear what these women had gone through and how they were struggling to overcome years of trauma and build good lives for themselves.

That night I went home and was hit with such a mix of emotions. That day was off the charts in so many good and really difficult ways. I found myself lying in my bed, unable to fall asleep, thinking about every one of those resilient girls who were struggling with the basics of having what they needed to get an education or something to wear to a job interview that would offer them a step up out of a shelter and into a home of their own. But mostly I was in shock, thinking about the forgotten girls whose dreams had been stolen from them, the girls escaping domestic violence and sex trafficking who had never been told they were beautiful and worthy of good things in life. The girls who had never felt loved and encouraged in a way that all girls deserve to be. The girls who felt that dreaming was for someone else.

I'd been told my entire life that I could do or be anything. I'd always had my family and friends behind me, cheering me on, and reminding me over and over that I am smart and beautiful and so loved. It absolutely wrecked my heart to see girls who had never been told any of that and who didn't believe that they were worth anything. This problem was so big and terrible, and these issues weren't getting the recognition they deserved. I prayed, asking God why more people weren't helping. *What is wrong with everyone? Why aren't other people actually doing something about this?* It hit me between sobs. A realization crashed into my brain like a wrecking ball, and my jaw—no joke—dropped open like in a cartoon, and my hands covered my mouth.

I was asking the wrong question. The right question was, "Why wasn't *I* doing something?" Why wasn't *I* working to solve this problem? Why was I waiting for someone else to take action? My heart was breaking for these women, and I was on my knees praying for them, but if I felt this convicted, then I should be out putting those prayers into action. I should be using my resources and my privilege, my closet and my extra time, to make a difference every day—not just for one random free shopping spree.

There was a part of me that came alive during that first free spree that I hadn't even known was in there. I think I had always been too busy focusing on my own grind, top-line sales and bottom-line margins, to give much thought to what I could be doing for my community. I occasionally felt guilty about not being a do-gooder, but I always had a ready excuse. I would get the store opened and then volunteer. I would get the loan paid off and then donate. I would get the second store profitable and then give back. My entire approach to my mission changed that night. I could use clothing for so many more people than just my customers. I knew something was brewing in my heart.

The next morning I woke up with a renewed spirit. Instead of feeling angry at all the people who weren't helping, I felt empowered to be on the team that was. Free fab'rik had been such a gift to the girls who'd attended, but there were so many more girls to serve. We hadn't even scratched the surface of this need. We had to do it again, regularly. There were a lot of options, and I wanted to explore all of them. It was such a thrill to open fab'rik and watch the business grow, but ultimately that was all about me—making myself happy, feeding my own ego, and focusing on my own wants and desires. I was actually a little tired of focusing only on myself. Helping women with free fab'rik felt like I had unlocked the best of myself—like a huge, new part of my heart was saying, "Put me in, Coach. I'm ready to play." I wanted to help more women feel beautiful through the power of an outfit. I wanted to hear more stories and connect those women with people I thought could help them. I wanted to facilitate job interviews and study groups and find new apartments. I wanted these girls to be able to dream again. My problems and struggles seemed so small in comparison, and I felt grateful for all I had in a fresh way. It fed my soul to be out there making a difference in others' lives. This is what people talked about when they talked about purpose. What a powerful and peaceful feeling it was.

WHAT BREAKS YOUR HEART?

The warehouse we'd rented still had donations sitting in it, and I'd been contacted by more organizations than we could fit in one Saturday. So we decided to do it all again. We called for more donations and volunteers, and I scheduled five Saturdays' worth of groups to come through. People kept bringing in clothing, and the warehouse stayed full. We focused on giving each girl who came in the same love and WOW experience we'd give to our fab'rik customers, but we did try to tame the chaos a little. Instead of a free-for-all of filling bags with as much as anyone could grab, we gave each girl ten tickets. Each item of clothing "cost" one ticket, and our volunteers helped each girl build a wardrobe of pieces that could be mixed and matched for different occasions.

Our free fab'rik mission statement came to us from Proverbs 31:25: "She is clothed in strength and dignity and laughs at the days to come." We hoped that clothing could be the catalyst for confidence and dignity and a reminder to dream big for the future. A pulled-together outfit was like armor, and these girls could now go to battle for themselves. We started to see that job interviews, court cases, and schools were places where women needed the confidence clothing could give to help carry them through, so we reached out to our fab'rik vendors to see how they could help, too. Once again, people rallied around our mission in droves. Our vendors sent boxes and boxes of new clothing and accessories. Because of that we were able to tailor different sprees to the pressing needs of different organizations.

We hosted a back-to-school spree for teen girls, where we offered brand new backpacks, tees, jeans, and sneakers. We sifted through all the donations to find khakis and polo shirts that could work as uniform pieces and even found some T-shirts, sweatshirts, and sweaters from different local schools so the girls could show their school spirit on game days. We offered a spree exclusively for moms, where we had tables of handbags and heels and racks of work-appropriate clothing and accessories. When working with safe houses and shelters for women escaping domestic violence and sex trafficking, we offered pajamas, sweatpants, and wardrobe basics like packs of new socks, underwear, and bras since most of those women arrived at the shelters with nothing but the clothing they were wearing. I was so proud of my community for the way they kept showing up for these women through free fab'rik. After six sprees the response continued to be overwhelming. How could volunteer slots actually have a waiting list? I knew that I had to find a way to keep free fab'rik going. I wanted to make it a permanent part of our business, but we couldn't keep closing our store every other Saturday. It was the biggest sales day of each week, and as much as I loved free fab'rik, I couldn't let it negatively impact the core part of our business. I was committed to finding a solution and making it sustainable, because once I'd seen the power of my newly discovered purpose in action, there was no going back.

That first free fab'rik spree cracked open my heart and let so much light and love in. It wasn't that I hadn't wanted to help people before. I'd volunteered with various organizations and donated to lots of worthy causes, but nothing had lit me up inside like free fab'rik did. I knew this mission had to be mine, because it was what broke my heart. Using clothing to help hurting young women who had given up on their dreams feel strong, beautiful, and hopeful for their future felt unique to me. It felt sacred. It felt like a hand-assigned responsibility that I couldn't turn my back on.

I believe that these are the women I'm called to help, that this is my purpose. Leaning into it made everything in my life brighter and clearer. Figuring out my purpose didn't overshadow my passion. Instead they amplified each other. I'd been living my dream before, but now I was living it in 3-D. Marrying this newfound purpose of helping hurting women with my deeply rooted passion for helping all women feel beautiful through fashion just lit such a fire inside of me. I only wished that I'd figured this out at the very beginning.

So here's a question that I wish someone asked me a long time ago: Do you know what breaks your heart? What is that thing that you see out there in our world that you can't believe hasn't been fixed? The issue or cause that, once you see, you can't unsee or pretend it isn't there anymore? If you've already found your purpose, then I hope you are chasing it with everything you've got. Keep going—I'm cheering you on! But if you haven't found it yet, I want to encourage you to start looking. I promise you, you aren't the only person who wasn't assigned one. It's just simple math—we need each other. Unfortunately, you aren't going to be able to thumb through a catalog and pick out a purpose. It's something already inside of you, and the people in your life likely already know what it is. They see where you donate your extra money or where you spend your extra time. They will remember the conversations where you squinted your eyes and could barely listen, and they will remember which stories you told that made you shake your head in despair and say, "I can't believe that happens."

I've heard some people say that passion and purpose are one and the same, but I just don't agree. Passion fuels you. Purpose fuels others. Passion may pay the bills, but purpose feeds the soul. Sometimes, if you are very, very lucky, you get both all at once wrapped in a pretty bow, but that's hard to find. For me, passion has filled me with joy and has been what I do, and purpose has filled me with despair and been what I'm called to do. The good news is that God has uniquely equipped each of us for our purposes over the course of our lives. You don't have to take classes or learn new skills—you come ready to rock. I really believe that God created me with a love of fashion and a heart for the hurting young women of the world, because my calling needed both of those components to make the biggest possible impact. Every life experience you've gone through, every strength and gift you have, and every relationship you've developed have been preparing you for fulfilling your purpose. I don't think God makes mistakes or says, "No purpose for this one! She's just going to wander around the earth haphazardly and not play the game of life."

Passion seems to grow from the things that make

you happy, using your natural talents and gifts. Purpose seems to grow from your own heartbreak, the challenges and valleys in your life. So often the things that break our hearts stem from the difficult things that we have overcome in our own lives. Lean in to those things. Be vulnerable, and know that we are all broken in different ways. I get that you may not want to spend all of your time thinking about them because, well, frankly, it hurts. That's a natural response, but you are stronger than that. It didn't take you down then, and it won't now. Push past it. Be brave, and step boldly into the past to use it for fuel for the future. Pour yourself into healing the hurt for yourself so you can use it for the good of others. It's the best therapy you can ever receive. When you've faced down dark things, God gives you a heart for others facing the same darkness.

IF NOT YOU, THEN WHO?

So how do you find your purpose? Once you know what breaks your heart, how do you put it into action and actually use it to help someone? I have found the best place to start is right in your own backyard. Open your eyes, and really look around your own neighborhood and community. What does it need? You'll be surprised at what you find. Look for organizations that interest you, and volunteer your time. You will know very quickly if the effort is linked to your purpose. It is like a light switch flipping on when what breaks your heart becomes clear. Just get out there, and get your hands dirty and in the mix of something. Your heart will either explode with conviction that this is what you were made for, or you'll cross it off the list. Remember, there are a lot of great organizations doing a lot of great things, but I'm asking you to find *your* one big thing. So while you may continue to be a part of many causes, don't give up the search for that special one. Keep trying until you find your thing.

You don't have to go so big and start a nonprofit like I did, but I will caution you to not go too small, either. Just dipping your toe in noncommittal waters isn't purpose. Purpose will often push you outside of your comfort zone. It's scary to be confronted by deeply broken and hurting people or suffering animals or injustices so intertwined with our society that they seem impossible to dig out. It will be easy to make excuses out of fear and let yourself off the hook. Do this too many times, and you stop chasing your purpose, instead looking at it occasionally from the comfort of your couch while you scroll through Instagram. But purpose is not online—it's on the frontline. When you're called, those excuses don't hold weight.

In theory, there was no cost to that first free fab'rik spree, but closing for a Saturday meant that paying rent would be very difficult that month. It was not a good business decision, but it was a good *heart* decision. When it comes to time, I have to call us all out. If the time we spent on social media, texting our moms' group, and watching Netflix was bottled up, we'd all have a lot of extra hours a week. Would you look one of the people you want to help in the eye and say, "I really wanted to help, but the traffic was bad so I turned around?" Would you look God in the eye and say, "I know you're nudging me to do those big things you made me for, but if you saw my Google calendar you would understand that I don't have time?" Heck no! Of course you wouldn't. So don't accept those excuses from yourself, either. Take a deep breath, and walk into this knowing you don't have all of the answers, and you don't know exactly how to help, but you know you have the heart to. Isn't the definition of "courage" being scared and doing it anyways? This is where bold comes out big time. This is where brave comes out big time. If not you, then who?

Our whole company shares our fab'rik purpose to make women feel beautiful inside and out, but many of the people who work for me have a deeper personal purpose, too. One of my past employees has a heart for unloved animals. She adopts elderly, abused dogs and gives them a home filled with love during their final days. She can only take one or two dogs at a time, so it might seem like she's not doing much compared to me saying our free fab'rik sprees have impacted over ten thousand women. But this woman is the entire world to those dogs! She cares for their every need, treats them how they should have been treated their entire life, and loves them unconditionally. Her purpose is literally life-saving. Don't dismiss any way to serve as too small. Sometimes it's the quieter, more personal serving that has the biggest impact.

When you start to look for your way to serve, you will see opportunities everywhere because God puts them in our paths on purpose for his purpose. He created you for this, so you can bet he's going to help you find it. Even if you are struggling with accepting it, even if you run away scared and screaming, he'll make sure you find your way back, and while it will be difficult, he will give you the peace you need to keep going. It hasn't been easy for me to sit and hear stories from sex trafficking survivors who have been handcuffed in basements for years or to talk to moms who haven't eaten in a few days so that their kids could. It hurts my heart and makes me question why God lets these things happen. Sometimes I want to cover my ears and run back to my cozy, wildly blessed life and forget that the bad stuff exists. But if we all did that, who would help those women? I know that God is using me, and while I haven't figured out all the details, I'm trusting that he's called me to this and he will provide what I need to succeed. He'll give you the courage to tackle the difficult stuff, too. Have faith, and commit. There is such power in hitting this tough stuff head on.

So what if you can't find an organization in your community that aligns with your purpose? Then maybe you are being called to create something of your own! You've looked around and figured out what the world needs. Now look at yourself, and figure out what you have to give. What are your resources?

What are you good at? Start there. Can you paint, cook, sing, organize? I'll let you in on a little secret: just about everyone wants to make a positive difference in the world. People want to help, but they don't know where to start. They are looking for someone to show them the way. When you're on fire for your purpose, they are going to be looking to you to show them the way—they are going to be counting on you to lead with heart.

I know, I know, this is a lot, but this is important stuff. I've now challenged you to find two really big things—your passion and your purpose. And that can feel like a lot of homework from one book. But it's worth the search. What if you got to the end of your life without discovering those things, and you didn't have the luxury of time to figure it out anymore? It took me years after discovering my passion and founding fab'rik to discover my purpose and create free fab'rik, and it took even longer to see how seamlessly they fit together. So don't be surprised if finding your purpose blossoms into something bigger than you ever imagined. And yes, I'll be right here saying I told you so!

So what are you waiting for? I hope you are not still looking around for someone else to solve the world's problems. If you think someone else is going to take care of your purpose and do the things you were made to do, think again. They're waiting for you to do it! Imagine how much brighter and lighter the world would be if every one of us was out there pursuing our individual purposes?

PURSUE PURPOSE

Guess what? The world needs you. You just need to figure out what cause you want to dedicate your time to. I believe the easiest way to figure that out is to answer this question: *What breaks your heart?* If you don't know, that's OK, but you can't know until you try and really *feel* it. So get out there and find out—it's your responsibility! If you think someone else is going to take care of it, think again. I think they are waiting for *you* to do it.

Time to carve out the space to pursue your purpose. Make a list of the causes you care about, and then make a list of a few places close to home you can go volunteer. Time to check in with your Wise Council. Ask them what causes they think you care about. When you have your list, it's time for action. I want you to take a step outside of this book—outside of the comforts of these pages—and go give your time to something. If the first one isn't it, try something else. It's out there, I promise. You just have to find it.

 CAUSES I CARE ABOUT

-
-
-

pursue purpose.

 PLACES TO VOLUNTEER

-
-
-

WISE COUNCIL TEXT: if I were going to start a nonprofit, what do you think it would be?

"What is that thing that you

see out there in our world

that you can't believe hasn't

been fixed?"

the sweet spot.

Once we had completed the first year of free fab'rik sprees, I knew that we needed to find a way to make free fab'rik a permanent part of our company. I had seen the incredible need around Atlanta, and there was no going back. Everyone was on board—we just needed to brainstorm and see how we could make the program sustainable. Shutting down our stores and pulling out all of our inventory, refilling the stores with donations, and then cleaning up and bringing inventory back in was going to wear us all out.

Having so much clothing and so many women in need, we decided to take another bold step in our mission to serve these women with a permanent location. We converted our first fab'rik location into a free fab'rik thrift boutique. It seemed to make perfect sense. We would have a place to set up all of the clothing, and instead of letting it sit in a warehouse between sprees, we could sell it and use the money to host free shopping sprees around the city. We partnered with a local organization to hire women from their program to work in the store. It was a great idea, in theory, but it just didn't work out. Stores have a lot of overhead, and five- to twenty-dollar thrift clothing didn't bring in large sales income, so we were struggling to support this part of the nonprofit while still remaining profitable enough to fund the free sprees, which were the real reason we'd opened the store. The free fab'rik thrift store that had seemed so purposeful was actually a distraction from our real purpose, but we learned a pretty important lesson: *Just because you can doesn't mean you should.*

You might assume I was frustrated or ready to throw in the towel at this point, right? Maybe I'd gotten my whole purpose wrong? We had clearly hit a dead end? Nope. Not at all! No one said this was going to be easy. It was time to redirect the GPS again. But we were now a little wiser and a little further down the road because we had figured out more of what worked and what didn't. "Stick to sprees, ladies," I heard God whisper with a wink.

As we were winding down on the thrift boutique, I went out and sat down with some of the incredible leaders of the organizations we'd been working with. They told me that a lot of the women that take refuge there are dealing with years of trauma and that going out into the world can feel very big and challenging. They also are working hard on recovery, so their days are filled with counseling, seminars, and prayer. As much as they may need clothing, the time to travel back and forth distracts from their rehabilitation, and they don't always even have transportation available. I immediately thought, *So why don't we bring the sprees to them?*

GO WHERE YOU'RE NEEDED

The first few times we set up free sprees in the safe houses were clunky and scary. We brought too many volunteers and not enough clothing. It was chaotic and difficult for people to connect. But we tweaked as we went. We whittled down the numbers until we landed on ten volunteers and ten girls. We used the living room space of the safe house that was the right mix of comfortable and functional. There were sofas and chairs, but we still had plenty of room to set up racks and tables of accessories. We tried different formats and finally landed on a flow that seemed to work well.

The night we really hit our stride was a rainy Thursday evening. I hosted a weekly small group with my closest mom friends from my sons' private school, so I invited them to join me on a free spree. These women all lived in Buckhead, one of Atlanta's more exclusive neighborhoods, and poverty and need weren't a part of everyday life for them. We carpooled over to the safe house together, and I could tell everyone was nervous as I drove down the dark streets. Many of the shops and buildings were boarded up, and the neighborhood was notorious for drug use, crime, and prostitution. It wasn't an area we would visit unless we had a reason. Tonight, we did.

"Are there any questions we shouldn't ask them?" one friend asked.

"Yeah, are they going to want to talk about their stories?" added another.

"What will offend them?" the third friend asked. "What if I say the wrong thing?"

I reminded them all that there are no expectations. We should simply be with these girls, let them know we are here for them, and treat them like we would each other. It was pretty quiet as we drove through the imposing iron gate and past the security guard.

Our volunteers were usually fab'rik employees or volunteers who'd been with us through several of our big free sprees, so they knew the lay of the land. This was my first time bringing in a group of all newbies, and it dawned on me that our volunteers were more nervous than the girls we were going to help. They were really stepping outside of their comfort zones, and I was so dang proud of them, driving into a clearly unsafe neighborhood, leaving their kids and security at home just because they wanted to help.

We pulled up to the house and waited for the House Mom to unlock the door. I guided them down the hall and started to explain more about what these houses do. I paused and brushed some lingering rain from my sweater, trying to pump myself up a little before I met the girls. For some reason, a wave of sadness always hits me pretty hard right before I go into these sprees. I guess it's a reminder of how the whole need for safe houses breaks my heart. I kept a smile on my face for everyone else, though, and continued to push the rolling rack down the hallway.

We walked into the living room, where were welcomed by one of the brightest lights in our free fab'rik world, my free fab'rik manager, Kayla, who exudes calm and purpose wherever she goes. I exhaled. For a temporary resting place for these women, the living room did a great job of feeling homey, with cheerful teal walls, inspirational quote art, fluffy rugs, and lots of cozy, beige sofas. Kayla and our volunteers prepped the racks of clothing, carefully laid out the jewelry on the table, and organized the shoes by size. I stepped back and looked at our pop-up shop. It looked like a boutique! The clothes were so beautiful that I wanted to shop it myself.

I felt ready, although my stomach was still filled with butterflies—partially from excitement and partially from nerves. It was the same feeling I got at the beginning of each marathon I'd run. I loved that feeling because it was proof I was doing something challenging, but so worth it. This was where free fab'rik belonged, in a safe room with the girls we serve.

I looked up as the door opened and the somewhat skeptical women slowly trickled into the room. A few gave us hesitant smiles, but many had arms crossed over their chests. They were closed off and reserved. I took a deep breath as the House Mom introduced us. She told them about free fab'rik and explained we were there to host a free shopping spree for them. At the mention of clothes, a few more smiles appeared.

"Hey, beautiful ladies, I'm Dana," I said cheerfully. "Come on in and get settled in on the sofas. I want to tell you more about why we are here." We all sat in a loose circle. I knew the minute we sat down that the girl to my right was having a really hard transition. She was painfully thin with dark circles under her eyes, and she just seemed so hopeless. Somehow, she gave the impression of almost disappearing into her threadbare gray T-shirt. She plopped onto the sofa, crossed her arms, and scowled at the room and then at me. It was clear she did not want to be there. Despite her tough act, I knew she was fragile and that we would need to tread lightly.

Putting that thought aside for the moment, I told everyone a little about myself, prayed for the night, and then broke out my secret weapon: a game called *Table Topics*. The game is basically just a box filled with interesting questions to get conversation flowing. I pulled out a card from the middle and asked the question to the group. "Would you rather live in the city or the country? I'd definitely pick the country because I'd really like to have a million goats!" My answer was met with a smattering of laughter, and then I nodded at the girl to my left to answer. We went around the circle. A few girls passed, and that was OK. My girl, the one on my right, passed every time by simply lifting her hand and shaking her head no. She didn't crack a smile at answers that had the rest of us nearly crying with laughter, and she didn't even look at the girls who shared some more painful answers. After about four questions, I could see the other girls all eyeing the racks of clothing and knew it was time to wrap it up.

"All right ladies, I know you are really here to shop. So pair up with someone you'd like to shop with, and let's go look at these clothes!" I immediately turned to my right. "Hey. Would you like to shop together? We have so much cute clothing over there!"

"I'm good," she replied, not meeting my eyes. All of the other women had paired up with our volunteers, so she and I were alone on the couch.

I smiled gently and tried again. Many of the ladies start with a wall, understandably, so sometimes it took a while for them to open up. "It's OK if you want to wait. It looks a little hectic right now anyway. Why don't I pull some things for you and we can go back in one of the rooms and you can try stuff on alone instead?"

She finally looked at me. "Can we just not shop and talk instead?"

"Absolutely," I nodded. "Yes, let's talk."

"So why are you here?" she asked. Her eyes narrowed into an accusatory glare.

I launched into my standard spiel about free fab'rik, but she clearly wasn't buying what I was selling.

"No, not why is this group here. Why are *you* here?" she demanded. "You talked about your kids and husband and, from how you're dressed, you probably have a fancy house. So what are you doing here with us on a Thursday night? Why aren't you home with them?"

I took a breath and thought for a moment. "I feel it's really important for me to be here. My husband and kids know it's important for me to be here, too. We're all women who are trying to get through life. We are all dealing with hard things, some surely harder than others, and I think we have to be there for each other. Today I can be here for you by bringing clothes and helping you pick out an outfit."

"No, really, what do you want from me?" she pressed.

"Honestly," I said, a little taken aback by that question, "I don't want anything from you."

"Everyone always wants something," she continued. "I've never met anyone who didn't want something from me. So what's your story?"

"What's your story?" I countered. I looked her right in the eyes and tried to project trust and love. There were all those other women having conversations around us—some laughing and being silly and others serious—but all the noise faded into the background, and that couch became a sacred space as we talked. I put my hand on her leg to steady her, and as she started her story, she placed her hand over mine.

She looked down as she said, "For the last few

years, I've been handcuffed in the basement of a nice hotel up north. No one knew I was there except this one guy, and every day and night, he would bring men down to have sex with me. People always want something. No one cares about me." Tears ran silently down her cheeks.

I went completely still. What do you say to that? What do you tell someone who's undergone something so horrific? So traumatic? What words or comfort could I possibly offer her? Her story almost snapped my heart in half, but everything inside me told me my strength was her strength right now, so I shoved my anger and disgust for those men into an internal box, took a deep breath, and trusted God to put the right words in my heart. "Do you know how brave you are?" I asked.

"It's not brave—it's horrible," she corrected me.

"Yes, it's horrible," I agreed. "But, right now, you are here on this sofa talking to me. That was yesterday, and here we are together today. You get to write a different story now."

That seemed to be the key to opening the floodgates. She poured out her story to me, and the details still haunt me today. I wanted to scream and rage and go hunt down every person who had hurt her to make them pay for what they'd done. But I could only put my arm around her and hug her. She didn't need me to fight for her. She needed me to offer her a space to grieve and to prove to her that there were people out there who wanted only to help, not to hurt. She needed me to show her unconditional love. When she looked up, I smiled. "I brought clothing. I can't offer much else, but that's what I have tonight. So let's shop. Let me bring you some things to try on."

She nodded and half smiled. That was enough. She wasn't ready to get up and go mingle, but she told me what she liked (black and denim) and didn't like (no bright colors!), and we bonded over our shared love of neutrals and hatred of pink. I found her a great pair of jeans and a three-quarter-length sleeve top in black and white stripes. We paired that with black and tan wedge sandals and a pair of delicate knot earrings. It was an amazing transformation. She went from ice cold to sweet and soft once we started trying everything on. At the end, we moved the tables and lined up chairs to create a runway. They all strutted confidently down to the latest Beyoncé song. I could tell my girl was a little nervous, so I taught her how to hold her hands on her hips and twirl midway. She checked herself in the mirror one last time and didn't hold back a smile. Then she walked out with her head held high and even struck a little pose as everyone clapped. After she left the runway, she walked over to me and hugged me. I hugged her back, the same both-arms, tight hug I give my kids, where neither person wants to let go. "Thanks," she whispered.

"No, thank you," I whispered back.

I checked back in with her the next time I came, but she was gone.

I still pray that she's safe, not on the street, and has

a job and maybe a family. But my bigger prayer is that she remembers that she is loved and beautiful and has so many people cheering for her. The work being done by these safe houses is incredible. They provide the physical safety and resources these women need to start the healing process. In contrast with providing shelter, food, medical care, and counseling, giving these girls an outfit may not sound terribly important. But the clothing is only part of it. Sure, we're giving these women a confidence boost with boots or a great skirt, but we're also bringing hope and showing them that there are people out there who care about them and their stories. We're giving them strength and support, so hopefully they can see a future without fear.

That night was, by far, the most personal spree I'd done. As I was lost in my girl's story, one of my volunteer friends was matched with a woman she recognized. They had gone to high school together. Watching them reconnect was really moving. It only took a few bad circumstances to cause their paths to diverge so dramatically, and it reminded all of us that any one of us could be sitting in a less blessed seat if a few things had gone differently. We're all broken, and we will all need each other to lift us back up. We all need grace and forgiveness and friendship and hope. We all need people to cheer us on.

WHERE THE MEANING IS

I felt like we'd finally hit our stride with our sprees, and my goal was to institute a weekly spree. We opened up each visit to allow for ten volunteers. At first, the volunteers were primarily fab'rik employees and our friends, but within a few weeks our customers learned about what we were doing and joined us. Now those volunteer spots fill up within the hour, even though we post them months in advance. I'm still in awe of how many women want to be part of free fab'rik, and I can't imagine what we would have missed out on if my closet rod had never broken.

Free fab'rik now happens two to three times a week in Atlanta. All of our stores collect clothing donations, and each store is matched with an organization in their city where they send their donations. Not every store goes into safe houses and does the community free sprees we do in Atlanta yet, but I love that there are over forty partners that can count on a steady stream of good quality donations from our fab'rik shoppers.

I never would have imagined free fab'rik growing to be so big when I dreamed of actually meeting the women I was donating my clothing to. It's like I blinked and my passion exploded into purpose, and they became one and the same. My heart started to beat in the sweet spot where they overlapped, using my love of clothing to take care of those I love who need me. There's no way I'd be making this large of an impact if I'd stayed safely in my own lane, going the speed limit, and just cruisin' straight ahead. I would have missed the point and the very best part.

I think a lot about what it will be like at the end

of my life when I meet God. I doubt he will ask me about my fab'rik P&Ls, strategic plans, and how many stores I had. I think he's going to want to have a cup of coffee with me and hear the stories of what happened when we brought a car full of volunteers down to meet these women in need, love on them, dress them, and show them his love. He already knows all my stories because he was there for every single one, but I'm hoping we will hug each other when I thank him for choosing me for this.

Then I hope he says, "I loved how you tied your passion and purpose together!"

And I'll laugh, point at him, and say, "No, no. I love how you did that!" Then we'll laugh together and high five.

I'm mostly kidding, but I do hope he will say, "Well done, my good and faithful servant."

ANSWER THE CALL

Finding your purpose is such a settling feeling. But just like with passion, the real work begins after you figure out what that purpose is. When you are called to do something, you actually have to *do* the thing in order to answer that call. How you do that work is entirely up to you, but one of the most powerful ways you can do this is to find ways to marry your passion and your purpose together—turn who you are, what you do, and who you want to serve into the same thing.

At the core of what I do, I try to use what I love

to make people feel loved. I use clothing to remind women they are beautiful and powerful and that they should never ever give up on dreaming big for their own futures. That's the legacy I want to leave, what I want my kids to tell people their mommy does. None of us will ever get it exactly right, but I do know with 100 percent certainty that there is a magic that happens when you start to live your life in the sweet spot between what you love and what our world needs. Imagine if your passion and purpose could cross over like mine, and you could spend your days in that sacred space where what makes your heart beat could help heal others' hearts.

Feel like your passion and purpose have nothing to do with each other? Try to see how they link together, anyway. Look for opportunities for the two to overlap. Prepare for it all to seem nonsensical at first. Just trust that it will all be woven together eventually, and know that forcing it isn't your job. Remember that we plot the course, but God directs our steps. So have faith and conviction, and check in with your Wise Council. Maybe they'll be able to see the thread that weaves your passion and purpose together even if you can't. Offer your passion up where you volunteer. Someone else in the organization might know of the perfect way to use you. Look for others who seem to be in their sweet spot, and see what you can learn. The right work to do for your purpose won't be something you hate doing. It should be something that energizes you—a way to pour out your gifts to others, where no matter when the "shift" is over, you could stay all day. You don't have to do charity runs if you hate running or sell candy bars door to door if fundraising isn't your thing.

If your passion is cooking and your purpose is helping the homeless, why not make trays of your signature dish and show up at the closest homeless shelter? (I bet there is one closer than you realize.) I have a beautiful spirit of a friend named Kitti Murray, who turned her obsession with coffee and her love for her refugee neighbors into Refuge Coffee Co., a coffee shop and de facto community center in Clarkston, Georgia, that provides living wage jobs and holistic job training, coaching, and mentoring opportunities to resettled refugees. Her coffee shop and coffee truck both serve as a gathering place where refugees can mingle with locals and foster relationships. How cool is that? She started out volunteering with World Relief and found her purpose creating a wider, more accepting community for refugees in her neighborhood, Refuge Coffee was born from that. And she did all of this in her late fifties—so it's never too late!

If your passion is being a mom and your purpose is helping those that don't have moms, you could write notes to the children in orphanages and girls' homes that never get that motherly love and encouragement. Remind them they are loved, and tell them all the amazing things you say to your own children. Have your friends write notes, and imagine how those kids will feel opening their mailbox to stacks of love notes. I've been there when orphans received letters like that, and I can't adequately describe the power of those words. Isn't that beautiful to think about? Someone had better go do that! (Wait, maybe it should be me?) If your passion is the law and your purpose is cancer research, ask if you can give a presentation to your organization. Companies are looking for their employees to infuse their company culture with heart. Trust me when I say that your commitment to a great cause will catch the attention of your bosses and your peers in the best possible way. Companies love to see employees caring about others this way, because it shows they have compassion, conviction, and courage, and everyone wants that person on their team.

Remember, there is no rule book to any of this. So much of this is faith and gut. You'll have to figure it out as you go, and it will be frustrating sometimes. Sometimes I get angry that more isn't being done, that it feels like we've only helped one hundred women this month and there are so many hundreds of thousands more. But! But! But! We've helped one hundred women. Those are one hundred precious lives that will hopefully be inspired to go on to find their own passion and purpose and help others after our time together. Those are one hundred precious women who have a chance to live impactful lives because I'm living one. Get it? Living in your sweet spot makes you shine bright, and you will inspire other people to jump on board, take action with you, or go take action somewhere else. Who knows how many people those one hundred women will go to help?

It's a domino effect. And that is huge when you think about it. Clothes might not change the world, but the women who wear them can and do!

SWEET SPOT

What would it feel like if what you loved to do, your passion, intersected with what the world needs, your purpose? What if that became the space where you lived and worked and spent your days? This can take time to fall into place, but this is the sweetest place in life.

Is anyone else excited about going through the process of seeing where your passion and purpose can overlap? I asked my parents this question on a long drive. It was pretty obvious they share the same passions: art and family. When it came to purpose, they have both always had a heart for abused children. They both admitted they hadn't really ever thought how those things go together. I had them captive for a six-hour car ride, so I pulled out my journal and had them brainstorm. Within ten minutes, they both had a list. Unsurprisingly, their lists were similar. My mom said she would love to have a kids' camp at their house (it sits on a few acres) for hurting children, and my dad said he would love to do art therapy for kids. Being professional dreamers, it didn't take long until they were describing a kids' art camp for abused children they could host in the summers at their home so children could come heal through art. It was so inspiring to watch them talk about this place they could create together. Something tells me I will be volunteering at their camp soon.

Your turn! Grab a sheet of paper and draw two big circles that overlap in the center. Write your purpose in one circle. Write your passion in the other. Now make a list of ways these two can combine in the space where the two circles overlap. It might take some brainstorming, but it will come to you. Remember: be creative, and don't limit yourself.

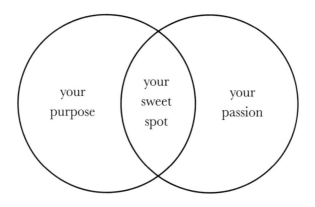

"What would it feel like if what you loved to do, your passion, intersected with what the world needs, your purpose?"

SEVEN

expand your heart.

I half-jogged down the hall, trying desperately not to twist my ankle in my probably way-too-high-for-church heels. I carefully opened the double doors in front of me and slipped into the crowded sanctuary and down the aisle until I spotted Angelo saving me a seat. We were running late as usual, and I had just managed to get Lincoln and Hudson settled into the nursery in time to make the service.

I reached over and grabbed Angelo's hand, squeezing it, and whispered, "Thanks for sitting in the front row, love. I know how much you hate it." He leaned over and kissed my cheek just as the lights lowered and the music began. When the song ended, I laid my head on his shoulder and he wrapped his big, muscular arms around me. I could feel the week's stress melt away as the words of the songs ran through my heart. I had a to-do list about a mile long in my bag, but for a few hours I knew I could forget it and just be in the moment. I loved everything about our church. It had become my happy place—the time each week that quieted my restless soul and allowed me to rest and refuel.

After the music ended, a video started. It was filled with footage of people on mission trips, digging wells, praying in circles, and holding babies. I reached down to pull my checkbook out before the second image had even left the screen. A nervous energy gripped me. I bounced my leg, trying to contain the need to jump up and *do something* about what I was seeing. My eyes didn't leave the screen. While I had seen videos like that before, this one hit directly into my heart like an arrow to a bullseye. A man shared his story on the screen, and it almost felt like a direct challenge. "Let me guess, you're sitting in your seat thinking you have a job, young kids, and responsibilities, and that you're just far too busy to go across the world to help these people. I get it. I've got a very busy life, too, with four kids, a demanding job, and a long list of commitments. I sat in your seat and was sure I didn't have time for a mission trip either. But God calls for us to care for those in need, and there are so many people in desperate need. I'm sure you are already doing good work in your community, but there is a whole world of people that need us. I want to urge you, encourage you, to sign up for one of the mission trips if you feel even the smallest calling. This will change your life."

I glanced over at Angelo to get a read on whether he was feeling what I was. We were going on a mission trip. My heart had already decided—I just needed to convince my husband. I started planning it all in my mind. How in the world would I pull this off with fab'rik growing like it was? I'd never even taken a vacation, much less gone across the world for a week and half. I had two little boys under age three. My parents would gladly babysit, but I'd never been away from them that long. Was it safe? Could we do this? How could we not? I leaned over to Angelo before the video ended and said "Babe, we have to go. I have no idea how but . . ."

Angelo interrupted my frantic thoughts and whispered in my ear, "Yes, of course we're going."

WHO WILL HELP?

I groaned audibly as I fell back on my little twin bed at the end of a long day. I ached everywhere.

"Tired, baby?" Angelo chuckled. He watched as I winced my way through unlacing my boots.

"Why am I so beat? I thought I was stronger than this." I knew I was whining, but I was exhausted. We'd been working all day to clear rubble, and it felt like we'd barely accomplished anything. Walking back and forth up the broken roads of Haiti with broken families staring at us and broken dreams thick in the air was harder than I had expected. Over 250,000 people were dead. Even more were injured, and over 1.5 million Haitians were unable to return to their homes. It was almost difficult to believe that the piles of rocks and debris had even been buildings—carefully tended shops and lovingly built homes. We saw children huddled together, crying outside of a former school, and tent cities made from bedsheets where young mothers tried to create temporary safe places for their little ones. My heart broke for those moms and those babies. Little kids played soccer in the street with a ball they'd made from trash. During our breaks, we'd jump in to play with them for a few minutes before we needed to get back to work.

"Come here," Angelo laughed. I did too, as I watched my big, strong, six-foot-three guy jump into my tiny bed with me. I cuddled up to his chest, and he leaned down and kissed my forehead. "We're doing good stuff here, Dana. I'm so glad we came."

"I know. It just doesn't feel like nearly enough." Restless, I pulled my journal and a pen from my bag and wandered over to the window, leaving Angelo to pull off his own dust-covered boots.

The view spread out before me was so jarring. That much destruction just didn't seem real. But I knew it was. I had spent all day moving rubble down there. I felt so inadequate, so ill-equipped. What had I really thought I could accomplish here?

"I'll be back in a little bit," I told my hubby as I wandered out the door to explore. I found stairs that led up to the rooftop and sat there to watch the sun sink low past the barbed-wire-topped gates around us. We were staying in the upstairs of an orphanage, and below me I could hear the muffled noises and cries of babies trying to sleep. I dutifully wrote down everything we'd done that day, trying not to cry, myself. I couldn't focus. The whimpers from below me seemed so loud in the quiet twilight. I squeezed my eyes shut and tried to block the noise out. All I could think of was Lincoln and Hudson, their chubby little fists clutching their blankets, crying and crying for me, not knowing I would never be able to come for them again.

The orphans below us didn't understand that their mommies and daddies were gone forever. How could they possibly understand the destruction that had unmade their lives in a matter of minutes? I couldn't even understand it or accept it, and I got to go back home in a few days to my electricity and running water, where I would hug my boys and send them off to a safe preschool and kiss them and hug them and tuck them in each night with full bellies and full hearts. Who was going to do that for these poor Haitian little ones? These sweet little souls that clung to us so ferociously when we picked them up? Who was going to love all of these untethered children?

WHY NOT ME?

The next day, we got to experience a Haitian church

service. It was hot and long, and of course I couldn't understand any of it since it wasn't in English. My mind drifted back to those children where we were staying. I couldn't stop wondering who would take care of them and love them and give them hope again.

"Why not you?" said a voice as rich and warm as honey. I felt it more than I heard it. Everyone else from our group was journaling and watching the service.

"Why not you?" I felt that voice again, so gentle and kind I knew it had to be God. I'd never heard God like that before. But here, in this deeply broken place, his voice was clear.

Adopt? We don't need to adopt. We already have two healthy little boys. Why would we adopt? But then the question became *why wouldn't we adopt?* I mulled it over in my head for the next few days, a little nervous to even tell Angelo. I couldn't come up with a single reason we couldn't adopt, but I could come up with a million reasons we should. We had the money and the space and so much love to give. Why not me? Why not us? The moment I thought it, all of the tension and grief I had been holding since we landed in Haiti melted away. I felt peaceful. A new fire was running through my veins.

As soon as we got settled back on the bus, I turned to Angelo and said, "Babe, we're going to adopt. We have to adopt. There are so many babies here without parents, and you can't go through life without a mom and dad, without a family. I know we're crazy busy, and I have no idea how we would pull this off. I know it takes years and people are going to think we are crazy with how chaotic our life already is, but I feel like God is telling me this. Please don't think I've lost it but . . ."

"Baby, I know," Angelo said gently, cutting me off. Then he laughed. "Remember, I've always wanted to adopt. You got so mad at me when I suggested it."

I felt myself flush. Dang, why is he always right? We were sitting at the bottom of his stairs on our second date, and I asked him how many kids he wanted to have. He said he wasn't sure, but was sure he would adopt. My vanity and pride took over, and instead of seeing his beautiful heart for forgotten kids, all I'd been able to think of was sweet, chubby baby boys with his olive skin, black eyes, and eyelashes or my blond hair and wild spirit. Now I knew—I just knew—that our family wouldn't be complete without a child that didn't look a thing like either one of us.

"You were right," I whispered. "You were right the whole time."

Angelo sat straight up, all traces of fatigue gone. He looked at me with wide eyes. "I think that's the first time you've ever said that me."

"And the last," I laughed as I playfully pushed him out of the seat.

That night when I heard the whimpers and cries of little ones trying to sleep, I clung tightly to the knowledge that I had been chosen to care for one of them. And if not here, then somewhere else, my child was waiting for me. In the meantime, I would hug them all so tightly the next day, let them fall asleep in my lap, and pray big for them all.

ON A MISSION

I came back from Haiti a woman on a mission. I had heard God speak to me. I had felt his spirit moving inside of me, and it changed my heart. I wanted to shout out what I'd learned from the rooftops. We'd been going to church for a few years, but it wasn't until I was sitting there in the midst of destruction and pain that I really, truly felt I was starting to know God. To me, he was no longer the be-good-so-I-can-make-it-into-heaven God or the do-your-best-so-I-can-be-proud-of-you-at-the-end-of-your-life God. He was this purpose-driven-voice-calling-me-to-be-a-warrior-for-others God. I wanted this God in my life, every part of it. I even Googled how to make fab'rik a Christian company. If there was a form to fill out or boxes to check, I wanted to do that. (There isn't. If you want to be a Christian company, as Angelo told me, you just be a Christian company—who knew?)

I was tired and jetlagged, but I couldn't get the image out of my head of this three-week-old baby girl from the orphanage crying and shivering because she had no one to hold her. I felt so convicted. I wanted those babies to feel the love they deserved, to know that we cared about them and that they had a future filled with hope. I wanted to adopt all of them, but

I knew Angelo was not going to let me go quite that far, so I decided to research whether it was possible to start an orphanage in Haiti. I looked into donating almost everything we owned and started to make plans for fundraisers to get the capital we'd need to build an orphanage. When I started talking about donating my car, Angelo sat me down and reminded me that I had a company to run, a one-year-old and a three-year-old, and a growing nonprofit with free fab'rik. Not having a car wasn't a real option for me. We both agreed that we had been blessed with so much that we needed to give back in equal part, but Angelo has and always will be my voice of reason. He had me breathe, slow down, check back in with God, and really figure out the best way to use our money and time. We decided we were going to start the adoption process on Monday.

We were up to our elbows in research on different adoption agencies and the specifics of adopting from Haiti and several other countries on Wednesday when I felt that exhausted feeling that I knew all too well. I jogged up to the neighborhood CVS and took a pregnancy test in their bathroom. I was pregnant. Wait, what? We'd always planned on having three kids, but I thought we would adopt our third. We definitely hadn't planned on having four kids! I felt so confused—I'd heard God in Haiti, but here I was in the CVS bathroom, knowing adoption would have to go on the back burner for now. Had I gotten it wrong? I thought God was calling me to adopt a baby, but maybe he was saying I was going to have a baby? I tried to put the idea of adoption to rest so I could focus on our third little one, but by that time it was too late. My heart had already fallen in love with a baby somewhere that needed us. We were still filling out paperwork and going through the process, but it all felt like a dead end for a while. It seemed like every turn was the world telling us this was a bad idea. Haiti slowed down on all foreign adoptions right after we got home because the government offices were all rubble. We looked into other countries like Columbia, China, and Russia, but we didn't meet the requirements, and to adopt in Kenya you had to live in Kenya for a year. I can convince Angelo of a lot, but quitting his law firm and moving to Kenya was a hard no.

Even though we were stalled out on adoption, I was barreling forward with my idea to build an orphanage. I wanted to call it Sanctuary. My initial plan was to build in Haiti, but there was so much red tape it became impossible. Africa was much more open, and the need was huge. All of my research kept pointing to Kenya. I started dreaming about the design as I fell asleep, just like I did when I was creating fab'rik so many years back. I could picture it in my mind: bunk beds, white cribs, an art and sewing studio, swings, and gardens. I assembled my Haiti ladies, who had been my Wise Council on our trip, and they all got behind it. We drew up the plans, met with friends of friends who'd done this, and started on fundraising plans. But then the record came to a screeching halt again. Turns out you have to be Kenyan to own land in Kenya and create the type of place I envisioned. Who knew? Clearly not me. I felt so frustrated. I was working so hard to do something good that would help so many kids, so why were doors closing instead of opening? Why would God tell me to do something and then send me on a wild goose chase? What was I missing?

I wasn't ready to give up, but I did have to take a break when I had my baby, a sweet little boy we named Ryder Christian. We had three healthy boys, and I was so blissfully happy being their mom. I had dreamed of having ten sons, and I had three, which most days felt a lot like ten. I should have been content with what I had, but my experiences in Haiti had expanded my heart in such a unique way that I couldn't forget all of those children who needed the love of a family.

HIGH STYLE WITH HEART

Of course, I brought my new heart for orphaned children into work with me. I couldn't help but pass this feeling of expanded purpose on to my fab'rik family. Watching how willingly they jumped on board with free fab'rik, I knew they'd be all in on this too. The women in my company are truly some of the most powerful combinations of insanely brilliant minds with insanely huge hearts. I decided to plan a fab'rik mission trip to Kenya. Right before Ryder turned one, Angelo and I headed to Africa with my leader-ship team, managers, and even some stylists and their significant others. I didn't require my team to use any of their vacation days, and they continued to be paid, because I wanted everyone to be able to come, re-gardless of their financial situation.

Going from fashion-focused to mission-focused was obviously a huge change for a group of high-heeled girl bosses who spent most of their days dis-cussing trends, sales, and celebrities. Watching these women, whom I already admired and respected, step out of their comfort zones, humble themselves to serve the poorest of the poor, and go joyfully without hair dryers and curling irons was one of the coolest things I have ever experienced. Seeing their hearts grow for the children and people of Kenya, I literally watched as our company mission statement changed from "High style. No attitude or sticker shock" to something that better encompassed our purpose as a company. On a bus travelling between villages, I wrote "High Style with Heart" in the margins of my journal, and the week I got back, that became fab'rik's new mission statement. We've offered a mission trip every year since.

We all came back from Africa wanting to do more to help the people there. Creating a fashion line seemed like a good way to combine our new purpose with our existing passion without taking anything away from free fab'rik. Kristi, our in-house designer, said she knew she could design a collection our entire company would be proud of. I wish you could all meet this girl. Her fashion sense is, in one word, stunning. However, stunning doesn't even begin to describe her heart. She has been a faithful volunteer in our church nursery for years, and her purpose is so clearly to care for babies. So we sat on the white linen chairs in my office one sunny day and dreamed what this line could be. Her designs were effortlessly chic, fashion-forward, and easy to wear. Since the whole idea of the line was to give back, for every dress we sold, we donated a matching dress to a woman in Africa. But it was a total failure. We didn't take African culture into account. Our effortlessly chic party dresses didn't make sense for African village life, where you needed to cover your arms and legs and walk miles for water. Making donations that people didn't actually need was pointless. So we went back to the drawing board.

Angelo and I were still slowly inching forward on our adoption. I knew I was going to name the child Asher, boy or girl. So I suggested naming the new line Asher to help keep that dream of adoption alive. Kristi was immediately on board, and she eventually proposed that the line benefit babies instead of women. Babies? Of course! I loved that idea. Just like with free fab'rik, it was important to me that we knew who we served. Instead of writing a check to an orphanage across the world (which I am so grateful that so many people do, so please don't stop doing that!), I wanted to make it personal for our team. I had seen the impact it had on them when they met the kids in

Kenya. With that in mind, we decided that each store would be matched with a baby from the orphanage we partnered with in Kenya, and the proceeds from their Asher sales would go to that specific baby. We put a picture of their sweet Asher baby in a frame in their store with the child's name and story. We wanted our customers to know these babies, too, and to share in our mission as much as possible. We pray for these babies when we are home and love on them when we are in Africa on our trips. Each store knows its baby's story and follows its baby's progress, and we celebrate big when each child is adopted. Maybe it would be easier just to write a check, but you can't put a price tag on the connection we feel when we fly over and actually hold these sweet angels. Our line's mission is to love on these little ones until they have their own families. The Asher line has been a living example of what happens when what you love overlaps with what the world needs. Our customers love it, and it is now sold in other boutiques outside of fab'rik, so this mission just keeps expanding!

In the midst of all of this, our adoption agent suggested we look at Ethiopia. We said yes right away. We had fallen in love with Africa. A few days before we left for our third annual fab'rik mission trip back to Africa, we got the call we'd been waiting years for. They had found our baby—an eight-month-old baby girl was waiting for us in Ethiopia. They e-mailed us her file and picture. I clicked on the e-mail's attachment and held my breath as her picture loaded. As soon as I saw her huge, dark brown eyes I knew she was meant to be mine. We were leaving for Kenya in a few days, and I couldn't bear the thought of being in Africa so close to her and not getting to meet her. Angelo and I begged our leader to let us make a stop in Ethiopia in the middle of our trip. I completed forms in triplicate and wrote checks like a mad woman to get the clearance we needed to visit her. I got everything in just in time.

A DREAM COME TRUE

A few short days later, Angelo and I landed in Ethiopia. A driver was waiting for us at the airport. His name was Yosef, and he was about the sweetest spirit I'd ever met. I wasn't sure how he would feel about Americans coming to take one of his own away. But he just kept thanking us. He led us out to his dinged up, ancient gray sedan with the windows permanently stuck down. An Ethiopian flag hung from the rearview mirror, flapping happily in the breeze. He tossed our luggage in the trunk, and we were off. Angelo sat on one side on the backseat, and I sat squeezed up next to him. We held hands and grinned like kids. We couldn't believe this moment was finally here. We had undergone years of required counseling on adoption, but nothing covers the "how you will feel when you are driving through Ethiopian streets to meet your baby girl" part. Yosef kept looking back at us with his huge smile. He pointed out landmarks and told stories of the villages we passed on the long drive out to Asher's orphanage. It was their rainy season, and many roads had turned to mud, so we had to drive into the brush and down some roads that I was pretty sure weren't really roads at all. I held my husband tight as we drove through what felt like an obstacle course of cows and donkeys, potholes, and debris. We didn't say much. I just stared out the windows, hungrily drinking in everything I could about my daughter's homeland.

The orphanages were built in discreet locations, so we had to drive through a maze of backroads, alleys, and makeshift paths to get there. On one side street, Angelo asked Yosef to stop. He'd spotted a little hut where a man was selling soccer balls and toys. Angelo bought up almost the whole lot. He'd realized sooner than I did that we weren't just meeting Asher—we were meeting a whole orphanage's worth of kids. And Angelo didn't want to walk in empty handed— he wanted to bring joy with him. A few minutes later, we pulled up in front of the heavy gates. Barbed wire topped the thick walls. We were flooded by little ones wanting to play, sing, and dance as we walked in. Angelo threw out the balls, and the boys went wild. The girls braided my hair, and one of the staff explained that they rarely saw blond hair and were fascinated by its soft texture.

"Are you ready to meet her?" the translator asked. I nodded, not trusting myself to speak. We were ushered inside to the main room and sat down. I was so nervous. Would she like us? Or would she be scared?

What would her personality be like? Would she laugh or cry when I held her? I wasn't sure my heart could take it if she didn't want anything to do with us. The room we were left in was the school room, and older children were singing to us and smiling ear to ear. They obviously knew why we were there, and what it meant to one of the kids upstairs. They came over for hugs, and within seconds we each had a lap full of kiddos nestled in our arms.

The singing continued, but my entire attention was on the door. When a nanny came down the stairs holding a bundled-up baby, I almost burst into tears on the spot. Was this her? She was this tiny little girl with huge, skeptical eyes, wearing knitted booties and a pink sweater. I had to fight down a sob of raw emotion. This was my daughter. They placed her in my shaking arms, and I held her close to me. I could feel she was a little scared and possibly fighting back tears too. Angelo wrapped his peaceful arms around both of us, and after a few moments, she sighed, leaned back, and fell asleep in my arms. I wanted to hold her forever. In that moment, I felt my heart grow bigger. That portion of my heart that had been on hold for four years just for her was filled. All of the anxiety I'd felt about whether I would love her as much as my three little boys at home melted away. It felt, to me, exactly like it had after I'd given birth. There was no doubt or question in my mind that Asher was my child. I marveled at her as she slept. Her limbs were painfully thin, and her belly was swollen and far too big for her tiny frame. Tears ran down my face despite the fact that I couldn't stop smiling. I whispered, "I love you, Asher," over and over in her ear. "Get ready for such a beautiful life, little girl. You've got a whole big family waiting for you at home."

I held her until she woke up, and I got another glimpse at those eyes and then passed her to patient Angelo, who couldn't wait another minute. Seeing him holding our sweet girl had me sobbing.

"Let's go, sweetie, I want to meet your friends," he said. He stood up and carried her upstairs to her room. The familiarity of her room and Angelo's spirit seemed to calm her and her playful personality broke through. Her room had about fifteen white cribs in it, with two or three babies in each. They reached out their hands to have us pick them up, and of course we couldn't resist. Angelo found a ball and played with Asher on the floor. I pulled out our Christmas card from that year and pinned it over the crib. I wanted her to be able to see her mommy, daddy, and big brothers smiling down at her every day until we could come back, which at this point was to be determined by the courts. The nannies tried to show me how to braid her hair, and I scooped her back up for more snuggles. The orphanage was hot and crowded, and I felt heartsick looking around at all the sweet little babies. Oh, how I wished we could adopt them all!

We only got to stay for an hour. It wasn't nearly enough time to absorb the dream that had come true. I put her in her crib and put my hands on her little face. "I love you, Asher. We will be back for you so soon," I said quietly through my tears. She pulled herself up on the edge of the crib, watching us leave with those soulful eyes. She didn't cry—most of the kids didn't—but I knew she didn't want us to go. For another twenty minutes, we kept going back to hold her one more time. Finally, the nannies recruited poor Yosef to come bring us back to the car. It was so difficult to walk out that door. We weren't just leaving her—we had to leave all the kids. I sobbed the entire way to the hotel.

I was wrecked. I don't think I've ever been that emotionally torn up. I was so filled with hope and joy that we'd met our daughter, but I was literally sick thinking of all of the other children waiting for parents who may never come. A piece of my heart was still in that cramped, impoverished orphanage, but I had to leave, go back to my life, and pretend everything was OK. It was far from OK. It was even worse when we got back to Atlanta. I thought about Asher every moment. I felt so guilty, and I prayed almost constantly. "God, please let Asher know we love her, that we didn't leave her, and that we will be back, hopefully soon. Amen." It became my version of the Lord's Prayer. I recited it over and over, while driving or running, cooking, cleaning, walking between meetings, and every night lying in bed until I finally fell into a restless sleep, my prayer still on my lips.

Six months later that prayer was answered in full. Angelo and I walked back into that orphanage, our steps light and our hearts overflowing, to bring our daughter home for good. We were told to expect medical problems, which was OK for us. We had checked the box that said "special needs." Her file suggested she may be HIV positive and may have malaria. We shuttled her to multiple pediatricians and specialists only to be told she was probably one of the healthiest and joyful internationally adopted babies they had ever seen. She was malnourished and needed some feeding up and extra care, but within a few months Asher was thriving. She's been the light of our lives ever since. She is funny and outrageous and so beautiful and kind. She adores her brothers, and having her as a sister has helped them grow and mature into more thoughtful, kind young men with hearts that beat for causes they may never have known about without her. She blew our whole world open and showed us all in a tangible way just how good God is. Our family was great without her, but it's complete with her.

When God nudges you, or flat out calls you by name, he's holding out a gift. He won't make you do anything. He made you for a specific purpose, but that doesn't mean you have to pursue it. A lot of people don't. A lot of people ignore those nudges and hold tight to excuses like "I'm too busy," or "I'll do it when the kids grow up," or "when I have more money." They say "no, thank you" to this beautiful gift of purpose.

Y'all, if I had said "no, thank you," to my purpose, I would have missed out on Asher. I would have missed out on Haiti and hearing God call me. I would have missed out on the love I have for my Kenyan family from my mission trips. I would have missed out on watching my friends and coworkers find their own pockets of purpose and grow into even wiser, more courageous purpose seekers. I could have pumped the brakes and just glided for a while, saying, "I'm doing enough." I could have ignored the nudge in my soul, dropped a check in the collection bucket for Haiti, and gone back to happily not thinking about destruction and babies without mothers. I could have used the work I was doing for free fab'rik and the I'm-too-busy card as my excuse, but then I would have never seen the bigger heartbreak of the world for myself. Our families and communities need us, but there is a big world that needs you, too. I could have collected the accolades for the good work I'd already done. I could have, but I didn't. Thank God.

Instead I said, "Why not me?" and flew to Haiti. I said, "Why not us?" and we said yes to adoption. I said, "Why not fab'rik?" and took us all to Kenya. God is offering you a gift. He's offering to lead you step-by-step up wild, wind-blown, rock-strewn, difficult paths that you can barely see. You have to walk on faith alone. But at the end? You'll find the most breathtaking views that put anything you've seen on Instagram to shame. He's offering you the chance to dance through this dark world, lit up with a fire from within. He's offering you the chance to live out what you were created for: a life filled with meaning. When you are living that life, your heart will keep expanding and so will your purpose. You won't be able to ignore the heartbreak that calls out specifically to you. Instead you'll answer, "Why not me?" and jump into the fray, ready to help those who need you.

EXPAND YOUR HEART

There is a long list of amazing things in my life that I never saw coming. At the top of that list are adopting a sweet baby girl, starting a nonprofit that hosts free shopping sprees, and creating a clothing line that benefits orphans in Africa. Because of my passion for clothing and my heart for forgotten women and children, all of these things have become part of who I am and what I do. It's time to time to think about your heart. Grab a blank piece of paper, and draw a heart.

1. Write your passion inside the center heart. This is your heartbeat, the engine that fuels everything you put out into world. For me that is clothing and the business I created around that: fab'rik, my passion.
2. Now draw a bigger heart around the first heart, and write your purpose inside. This heart is about your neighborhood. As I realized that I had way too much extra clothing and identified needs in my community, my heart expanded beyond my passion into my purpose, to the needs of those around me. This is when

I created free fab'rik.

3. Now draw a bigger heart around the second heart. What will go inside this heart? You don't have to have the answer right now. But as you continue to pursue your purpose, your heart will naturally expand. Dream big here, and think globally. I filled my third heart when I created the Asher clothing line and fab'rik's annual mission trip to Kenya.

Here's mine:

Asher Clothing Line

free fab'rik

fab'rik

"When God nudges you, or

flat out calls you by name,

he's holding out a gift."

EIGHT

burnout.

One of the hardest things about life is that you can be doing big, important, amazing things that light you up, and you can still stall out. For a few years, I lived a really full life on empty. What does that mean? Well, basically, my life was so full that I didn't have time to take care of it. My phone was always at 1 percent battery life, and so was I. I ran out of gas so often that I actually got used to continuing a conference call while ordering an Uber, riding in the Uber to a gas station to fill up a little red canister of gas, and then riding the Uber back to my car, and continuing on to work. Who lets that be their normal? I was the definition of running on empty, but from the outside you'd never know. I was burning out, but I hid it really well, even from myself.

Everyone gets to a point in life where they feel stuck, uninspired, and exhausted. It's a universal experience. You feel like you are running in circles instead of running straight to what's next. The things that used to bring you joy and fire you up become a burden. You find yourself short-tempered and frustrated with things that would normally make you laugh. And happiness and contentment become so elusive that you start to forget what they feel like at all. These are all signs of burnout. There is minor burnout, that you can bounce back from with a small break or a change in your routine, and then there is public, fall on your face, can't just shake it off burnout. No three-day weekend vacation or girls' trip is going to fix big burnout. That's where I was.

I ran fab'rik as founder and then CEO for fifteen straight years. I rarely took vacations or even days off, not because I couldn't, but because I didn't want to. I loved what I did. I have four kids, but I only took one real maternity leave when we adopted my daughter, Asher, and many days she was my sidekick at fab'rik as we were growing the business. I was on my laptop and taking calls with my newborn babies snoozing beside me. Date nights turned into logistics meetings to sort out Angelo's and my conflicting travel schedules. I was working on potty training while working on our spring marketing plans. I reviewed quarterly goals while my boys were scoring goals on the soccer field. I was a multitasking queen. I loved everything about being a wife, mom, and fab'rik founder, and I thought if I could just push myself hard enough, find another hour in the day, I could be all things to all people. But even if I hadn't had kids, running a business is just no joke, and every single thing about fab'rik, home, and my family mattered to me. I worried about forgetting an employee's birthday as much as hitting daily sales goals and about WOWing customers as much as not having fall trends on the floor in time. Nothing was not important to me, so it all became priority. In the beginning, I was my only employee, so I had to do everything. I was the salesperson, accountant, maid, buyer, marketer, and customer service expert. As we grew, I don't think I ever fully got the memo that I could let go of most of those jobs. I hired an amazing team, but I was still working with the entrepreneur, start-up, it's all on my shoulders mentality. It wasn't unlike me to pass on sleep, yoga, and even drinks with my sister in favor of doing more at work. The irony was that these were the things that kept me inspired and happy and fueled my soul. I had stretched myself so thin that you could practically see through me.

I was burning out, and I didn't even notice it happening. I was in every meeting, at every game, reading every book and every e-mail, and on every call, but I wasn't really there—I wasn't present. The saddest part of all is that I was losing the "love" part of loving what you do. All I could think of at any given moment was all the work I wasn't doing, all of the items left on my to-do list, and all of the people I was letting down. When I was at work, I felt the weight of what was waiting at home, and when I was at home, I felt like I wasn't there for my fab'rik girls. I became the friend no one could count on, which went against my very nature. It happened so gradually that I didn't notice it for a long time, the joy slowly leaking out of my days. Buying trips went from being my favorite thing to something I dreaded seeing on my calendar. Creative meetings to discuss marketing and trends went from time I relished to events I needed three cups of coffee to get through. And dreaming? Forget it. I would sit there staring at my journal, without a single thing to write down other than the list of stuff I had to do. Not being able to dream should have sounded every alarm and raised every red flag, but apparently I was too burnt out to even notice. If I allowed myself to feel any glimmers of dissatisfaction, I immediately assumed that I needed to give more, push myself harder, be better. I wanted to be superwoman, to do it all at home and at work for my employees and my kids because I loved them all so much. I had forgotten the wise wisdom they dish out on every flight: *You have to put the oxygen mask on yourself before you can help others.* I could barely breathe, and my oxygen mask was lying, forgotten, on the floor. There wasn't a minute of my day that was free or unaccounted for. The name of the game was productivity. My motto was "I'll sleep when I'm dead."

Our last quarter numbers were down at fab'rik for the first time in a long time, and I felt the pressure intensely to bring them back up. The success of our company meant a lot to a lot of people, so I couldn't just say, "Let's ride it out," like I would have when it was just me. I owed it to my employees and store owners and fab'rik shoppers to get those numbers up. I didn't have any margin to get out ahead of it, cast a new vision, and then have the team execute it. I didn't have time to sit and listen to my stores and all of their ideas for how to grow because—yep, you guessed it!—I was too burnt out. fab'rik meant so much to me and, now, to so many other people, too. I felt so much pressure on my shoulders to keep it going and to push it to new levels of success that I completely overburdened myself. I wasn't sleeping, and I wasn't happy, but I was too tired to even notice what a huge problem that was in and of itself. What had been my dream became my burden. It was heartbreaking. I was failing myself and the company that I loved so much, but what was the other option? I would never quit, never give up. I was in denial. I clung stubbornly to my superpower and insisted that everything was fine. I had it under control, thank you very much.

As you can probably imagine, burnt-out-but-totally-overcompensating-for-it Dana wasn't particularly fun to work for or with. The more thinly stretched I became, the more I felt out of control, which in turn made me want to control things even more. I didn't have the time to fully hear about a problem, so would propose a solution that was more of a Band-Aid than the surgery the problem really needed. I was high on expectations and short on praise because I was running on 1 percent battery life, and I had nothing left to give. I was leading on empty. I didn't take time to encourage my team, celebrate their wins, or pour into their growth and development. I only had time to bark out what they could do better. I didn't have it in me to travel to my stores and be on the floor to remember how difficult it can be trying to make sure customers are happy, run a store, and inspire a team. So I didn't have enough empathy for what my team was going through. I had forgotten those early days in the store and had replaced that knowledge and passion with spreadsheets, sales goals, and budgeting. I'd dug myself so far into the process side that I forgot to look up and praise the people who were carrying this dream with me.

TOO MUCH

I knew things weren't good, but I clung to the idea that if I could just get through this difficult stage, I'd get back to happy and the fearless leader I used to be. Then came the straw that proverbially broke the camel's back. Angelo was presenting at a conference on St. Simon's Island, and he asked me to come with him so we could turn it into a little romantic getaway after his speech. We'd both been working so much that we felt like ships passing in the night. A marriage is like any other relationship—both people have to pour into it to keep it going strong, and we had both been taking that for granted. We needed this trip to help us slow down a bit and reconnect.

While Angelo was presenting, I slept in until 8:00 a.m. (unheard of for me!), went for a run, and then decided to check my e-mail before my massage appointment. I had an e-mail about some reviews for fab'rik on a company review website. I'd never looked at those before, but I was intrigued, so I clicked on it and saw a link to a review that would change the next year of my life.

It was an anonymous review, but I knew instantly who wrote it. It was from someone I had trusted implicitly, someone very close to me, and it was heartbreaking. I was shocked that someone would actually write something like this. I saw another review and decided to read it too. And then another. And another. I sat, reading, with my hand over my mouth and tears streaming down my face. I called Angelo before I remembered he was presenting and couldn't answer. Then I called my sister, Erin. I read the review to her amid sobs. They called me out by name, and there was even one review that suggested I'd adopted my daughter for social media attention. They questioned my faith, said my husband funded fab'rik, called me a bad CEO and a terrible mom, and said I didn't have any time for my team, that I was never there, and that I was catty and vindictive. Erin consoled me until Angelo walked in.

I asked him to read the reviews, and I laid in bed, curled up in a ball, and watched while he sat and took it all in. I was in shock. Would he agree? Did he think these things were true? After he finished reading, Angelo said, "How could anyone ever say things like that? You know they aren't true, don't you?" At that point, broken and all confidence lost, I didn't know who I was. He gathered me in his arms, and I cried until there weren't any tears left. I felt like I was having a panic attack. Not because someone had said something mean about me, although that hurt for sure, but because I knew that there was some truth amid the lies. I mean, adopting Asher for social media? Who would even think that—let alone say it out loud? There was nothing true about that. But there was a thread of truth woven through those reviews that rang out loud and clear to me. I had not taken enough time for my team, my people, the ones that were helping carry my dream. I had made them feel underappreciated by the weight of my expectations and lack of praise for all that they were doing. That truth hurt more than the lies.

Those reviews brought an awareness to the surface—a hard, bitter pill that I don't think I was ready to swallow. When we got back, life hadn't slowed down, so I jumped back in at the same pace and pushed those reviews aside instead of processing them. I just didn't have the courage yet. What I didn't realize was the impact those words were having on my confidence, my spirit, and the way I was leading my company. I began to question myself, overthink everything I did and everything I said, and I don't think my confidence level has ever been that low. I was walking on eggshells in the company that I'd built. I wondered if I had ever been good at anything, despite the evidence of my success right in front of me. These doubts and horrible thoughts circled around inside my head on a constant loop. They were a bitter chorus that I couldn't escape. I didn't voice this to anyone—not my sister, not my husband, not my best friend, no one on my Wise Council, not even my mom and dad. I needed to be the strong, smiling face of fab'rik and the mom who was pulling it all off, so that's what I was going to do, even though inside I was crumbling.

A few weeks later, we booked a babysitter for a much-needed date night. I grabbed Angelo's hand as we walked through the doors of one of our favorite neighborhood restaurants and pulled him over to a table in a quiet corner of the bar area. While he went to get drinks, I hopped up on a stool, smoothing the skirt of my black dress down over my legs. It was so rare for us to have a date night, to be out on a Saturday night alone with nothing to do but focus on each other. We were supposed to be meeting a big group out for a friend's birthday, but I had made an executive decision and told my friend we couldn't make it. I need some undivided one-on-one time alone with my husband.

I held up my hand to cover a yawn. It had been a long week. They had all been long weeks lately. Long days melting into long weeks melting into even longer months. I wondered if I could take a cat nap there at the table while he got the drinks. Maybe no one would notice? Angelo returned moments later with perfectly chilled Moscow Mules in hammered copper glasses— what can I say, that man knows me so well!—to find me in the middle of another yawn.

"Tired, babe?" he smiled. I nodded. We both knew I hadn't been sleeping that much, but I don't think Angelo realized just how little energy I was running on. He'd been travelling a lot, so he hadn't seen the all-nighters I'd been pulling. I hadn't wanted to burden him with my problems, so I hadn't been communicating my feelings at all. Not being my usual open, honest self with my husband was making it difficult for us to connect like we usually did, especially since we'd both been travelling practically nonstop. I could feel us drifting apart a little, and it was killing me. Holding part of yourself back is not good for any marriage.

Angelo sat next to me, and I inched my stool closer. I suddenly felt like I couldn't get close enough to him. I threw my legs over his, practically sitting in his lap. I put my arms around him and leaned my head on his shoulder. He told me about his week, and I told him about mine. I told him about sending Ryder to school wearing only one shoe and that Asher wore a Cowboys jersey with a tutu one day. We laughed as I told him about the sweet notes Lincoln leaves on my pillow when Angelo's out of town so I don't get sad, and that I thought Hudson might be starting to have crushes on girls! Man, do we love our kids.

"Remember when we used to dream about all this stuff? We'd sit on date nights imagining what it would be like to have dream jobs and kids and a home and spend time in Africa and try to change the world? Remember?" I asked as I stared up to the ceiling and rested my chin in my hand.

He nodded and took a sip of his drink with a far-away smile on his face that told me he knew exactly what I was talking about.

"Well, here we are," I said. Finally, we were quiet for a few minutes, and then I whispered, "Babe, I know it's all good stuff, but it's just too much." I couldn't believe I'd just said that. Was I tapping out? Admitting I couldn't handle it all? Would he be OK that I wasn't superwoman? Was I ungrateful to have everything I'd ever wanted and not be able to handle it all? With so much, why was I so unhappy? The unbearably loud buzz of lies swirling around inside my head was still there, but the volume had been muffled just enough for me to admit that.

"Ok, then let's change it," he replied with this quiet confidence that made me fall completely in love with him again in that second. "I'm all in. Do you have a plan?"

"Not yet," I said.

"Well I'm not going anywhere, so we'll figure it out together," he said.

I gave him a small smile, but I was really thinking, *Where am I going to find time to do that?*

ARE YOU OK?

It was a typical Monday, fast and furious and full of overlapping meetings and "do you have a minute?" conversations that all took way longer than a minute. Lisa Dimson, fab'rik's Chief Marketing Officer, slid my office door open and leaned in with her bright, conquer the world smile and long, shiny, black hair. "I carved some time out for us today to have coffee offsite at 12:30. I want to try some positive disruption to our usual meeting routine."

"Perfect" I said. I figured I should Google "positive disruption" before the meeting, but it had the word "positive" in it, so I was in. I was really just thrilled she'd asked me to have coffee. No one ever asked me to have coffee—actually drink it and talk about life. They either have bad news or they want to "pick my brain," which sounds exhausting in and of itself. Coffee and conversation, even work conversation, outside of the office sounded heavenly. I was working on three hours of sleep, and I needed the caffeine boost.

I hadn't gotten much sleep the night before. I'd been worrying about the surgery my mom was having that day. A few days earlier, out of the blue, she'd lost sight in one of her eyes. I glanced down at my phone. No word from Dad yet about how the surgery had gone. I glanced down at my to-do list. I had four meetings, two conference calls, and six e-mails I really needed to respond to in the next few hours. I had promised a friend I would call her back since she was navigating some terrible marriage news and needed someone to listen. Angelo was out of town, and I had to get the kids to guitar lessons and football practice somehow. I really needed this day to go smoothly, because I wasn't sure I had it in me to deal with something going off the rails. So yes, coffee sounded perfect, but wine sounded even better.

Twenty minutes later, I found myself settled into a cozy booth with Lisa in a nearby restaurant. We'd made it inside just in time. Clouds had moved in surprisingly quickly, and the sunshine had turned into a deluge of rain right as we pushed through the door, laughing from sprinting across the parking lot in our heels. We settled in, and I glanced at Lisa over my menu as she nervously moved her purse around. I sighed. This wasn't going to be a "let's catch up" coffee—this was going to be an important conversation. While I'd never gotten around to googling the definition of positive disruption, I could feel there was something heavy on her heart. We ordered espressos and dove right in.

"So, what's positive disruption?" I asked.

She explained that her husband, Robert, had been talking about ways to break up your routine to disrupt old patterns to let in new, more positive habits. Then she took a deep breath and said simply, "So I hope you don't mind me asking, but are you OK?"

I froze. I couldn't remember the last time someone had asked me that. I was expecting Lisa to give me bad news, not ask me how I was doing. She went on to tell me how much she cared about me and fab'rik and that she could see that I was carrying too much on my shoulders. I almost answered, "Of course I'm OK!" but something told me Lisa could handle the truth, and I was so tired of pretending to be OK.

"No," I said with a tight smile. "I'm not OK, but you know that." Tears began streaming down my face immediately. Once I started talking, it all came pouring out. I told Lisa how stressed I was, how much pressure I was under, how heartsick I was. I explained how much I was struggling to be all things to all people. How I felt I was failing as a CEO, a leader, a wife, a friend, a daughter, a sister, and a mom. I told her that I didn't know if I loved what I was doing anymore and that it terrified me. I felt like I was treading water, barely keeping my head above the waves, and had been for about a year, but I just didn't know how to get back to shore. My job was to inspire and encourage, and sharing that I was burning out was not very inspiring. I loved fab'rik with every bit of my heart, but it was changing, and so was I, and I didn't know my place in it anymore.

I don't think any of that was what Lisa had expected, but she listened so intently, nodding in empathy and taking in every word. As I wiped away my tears, the storm broke outside and beams of sunlight began to filter through the clouds. It felt like a sign, and it wasn't lost on us.

"Did that really just happen?" Lisa asked, gesturing to the window. We both burst out laughing. The pressure had lifted, and it felt so good to laugh after the tears.

Finally, Lisa asked me, "Can I offer you a sabbatical?" She'd known someone from Nike that had just taken one, and it popped into her head as I talked. I'd never even considered that. I'd always been fab'rik's mom, and moms don't get time off.

"I don't think I'm allowed to do that, am I?" I asked. Lisa gently reminded me that I owned fab'rik, so I could do whatever I wanted. We talked through some of the details and came up with a basic plan. There was no rule book for this, so we were just going to have to make it up as we went. But just acknowledging that I needed a break made everything feel lighter.

"Do you think you will be able to do this?" Lisa asked.

"Absolutely," I said. "Do you think *you* can do this?"

"Yes. The team and I have got this," she assured me. "Do you trust me?"

"One hundred percent," I said firmly. I felt like we were blood sisters promising to have each other's backs through thick and thin around a campfire instead of two women making a business decision in a booth at JCT Kitchen.

"So when should we start?" she asked.

"Tomorrow?"

We both laughed. The kind of catch-you-off-guard giggles that you sometimes get when you are not sure what else to do.

"This is not how I thought this conversation was

going to go. I thought I might get fired," she admitted.

"Nope," I said. "Not even close." I looked at her in her "Do What You Love" tee being so brave and selfless, and I remember thinking, *You may be saving my life right now. How did you know?*

As we headed back, she asked me, "How do you feel?"

"Loved," I said.

I'm so grateful for Lisa for being willing to throw me a life preserver when she saw me drowning. She wanted what was best for me, for my team, and for fab'rik. She was willing to risk her career to do the right thing, speak the truth, and hopefully positively disrupt the course we were on. She told me later that she felt the Holy Spirit nudge her to have that conversation with me, but that she was very scared she would lose her job by doing so. I could see how anyone would feel intimidated to have that conversation with me, since I've never been great at taking criticism, but I've never felt so loved. And no, she didn't get fired. Instead, I made her acting CEO in my absence. She basically said, "Take a break, no questions asked, and our team will stand strong for you as long as you need." Having people like Lisa in your life is crucial to success. Others might have just watched me crash and burn and roasted marshmallows on the bonfire, but our Wise Council peeps won't. They will speak up and step in, even when it's news that's difficult to hear. People who will put themselves at risk to help right your course are worth their weight in gold.

And yes, there is something to be said for timing here. I'm sure many other people tried to have a version of this conversation with me, but I wasn't ready to hear it. I was finally ready—beyond ready.

BREATHING ROOM

Even though I needed the break desperately and I trusted my team completely, it was still really difficult for me to walk away from fab'rik, even if I knew it was only temporary. There was such a sense of guilt and abandonment. Moms don't leave their kids, and fab'rik was my very first baby. Taking that sabbatical felt like what I imagine it would feel like to hand over my actual child to someone else for a month so I could rest and focus on myself. It felt irresponsible and wrong at every level. I would miss fab'rik so much and feel so lost without caring for it and shepherding it, but I also knew that I couldn't go on like this. I needed the space to refuel. I was like a shell of myself, just empty and fragile. If I didn't fill myself back up, I wasn't sure what would happen, but I didn't want to find out. I didn't want to lose my fire and passion for my company, but I could feel it had dimmed. Taking time off wasn't a punishment or a penance—it was a gift from my loving team, and I was deeply grateful.

Before I left, I went through my e-mail and delegated everything I could. Then I deleted the rest. Yep, you read that correctly. I deleted 300,000 unread e-mails in my inbox. And nothing bad happened! It felt so wrong but so, so right. Then I had my team disable my e-mail address. I know myself, and if I had access, I would use it. I had to be all in or all out, cold turkey. We also decided that I wouldn't go into the stores at all. I set that rule and couldn't believe those words could possibly have come out of my mouth, but I knew it was a guardrail I needed to not get sucked back into the addiction of my amazing company. I unfollowed every fab'rik social media account. I'm not going to lie, it was difficult. For the last few years, I'd fallen asleep most nights scrolling through fab'rik's Instagram, liking items, only to wake up them being delivered to my front door by someone from my amazing team. Yes, that is a WOW! I was going to miss everything about fab'rik—every single little thing.

I basically went through withdrawal during those first few days—I was detoxing from my own company. I wanted to know what was happening so badly. But each day got a little easier as I slowly began to feel like a real person again. I had been in too deep for too long, and I desperately needed to regain a healthy perspective. I needed to look at my company and my life from the outside and get my footing again.

A few weeks into my sabbatical, I felt brave enough to return to those awful reviews that had taken the wind out of me the year before. I had printed them out, put them in a folder, and saved them for when I knew I'd be strong enough to read them with an open heart. I played Matt Kearney's latest album, made myself a fab'rik latte (our signature latte made of dark Ethiopian coffee with frothed SO Delicious Hazelnut creamer)—those weren't off limits!—and sat down with the folder. I opened it up and started reading word by word, page by page. I got through them all without a tear. Those words had lost their power. It was amazing what a little breathing room could do for my resilience. I decided to make three lists on three separate pieces of paper:

1. Things I could do better
2. Things fab'rik could do better
3. Not true/Hurtful

I wanted to focus on becoming a more effective leader during my sabbatical, and I knew figuring out how to handle this criticism would be a big part of that. I was actually excited to work through the difficult stuff, and I discovered that what broke me a year ago was inspiring me now. When I finished, I crumbled up the hurtful list and threw it across the room into the trash can as my dogs, Cowboy and Vader, watched. "She shoots, she scores!" I cheered.

When I looked at my remaining two lists, I noticed a common theme. A lot of the reviews were fueled by the lack of time spent with the people who needed me most. When I got back to fab'rik post-sabbatical, I made solving those issues a priority for myself and with my team. One of the biggest complaints was that I was never available to listen and encourage my stylists at the store level, so shortly after I returned, I went on a "Love What You Do" tour to visit my stores and meet with the owners, teams, and customers. I sat with them and learned what they loved about fab'rik and what they needed from me, and for the first time in years, I actually heard them. I took all of that feedback and created our Love What You Do Council. I wanted to make sure that we created a corporate culture that promoted refueling and helped keep people from burning out. I hoped my team would never have to make the same mistakes I had. Council members were nominated from all over the company and voted in. The council has focused on inspiring and encouraging our teams to not only do great work, but to love what they do. We've built a stylist growth path, made celebrations of birthdays, anniversaries, and hitting big goals a priority, and been able to hear the hearts of our teams through the council. We try to keep a pulse of what our team needs so they are operating with a full battery life and full gas tank.

THE BIG PICTURE

No one plans to burn out, but I think maybe we should, because it happens to *all* of us eventually. When it happens to you, you'll find yourself sitting amid the wreckage of a life you're struggling to recognize, with no idea how things got so off course. There are only a few options when you find yourself there. You can choose denial, smile and insist that everything is fine, and pretend that if you don't admit it no one else will notice even when everyone around you can see that the ship is sinking. Good luck with that option. Then there is the woe is me, feel sorry for yourself option where you just give up and wait for things to magically get better with no effort on your part at all. Yeah, sorry, that doesn't actually work and will probably make it worse. Finally, there is the get off your butt, take control of this thing, and dig yourself out of it one day at a time approach, where you actively rest, take care of yourself, and intentionally look for new ways to inspire yourself. We all know that's the best option, right? We should hit the reset button, pour inspiration back into our veins, and come out swinging, ready to conquer the world! (However, do keep in mind that burnout is not the same as depression. Depression is very serious, and if you suspect you are suffering from depression, you should be gentle with yourself and consult a trusted source immediately).

Maybe you've never felt burnt out from the day to day or overwhelmed with the fast-moving train of life, but I'd still encourage you to tuck away the lessons from this chapter so if life ever starts to race this fast, you don't repeat my mistakes. I hope my story can help you see burnout coming so you can right your course and not suffer through it. But my guess is that you *do* know what I'm talking about here. Around the time I was burning out in bonfire-level flames, a local paper was doing an article about me, fab'rik, and how I had it all (ha!), but instead, I opened up to the reporter and told her the real story. The revised article was called "The Pitfalls of Having It All," and it outlined, in great detail, the struggles that I was navigating. The day it came out, I got a round of applause and endless hugs in the carpool line at school. Moms and teachers were actually cheering for me for saying what so many of them were feeling. I still get plenty of e-mails from people in the same place, desperately trying not to burn out, trying to be everything to everyone, not having enough time to take care of themselves, and feeling like slaves to their to-do lists. When I tell people at dinner parties that I took a sabbatical, there are always so many questions. *Why did you do it? How did you do it? What did it feel like? And did it work?* Just knowing this is such a common conversation is pretty telling about how rampant burnout has become.

I burned out because I was trying to do it all, all by myself. I had to come to terms with the fact that I can do *anything*, but I can't do *everything.* But too much certainly isn't the only way to burn out. Too little is just as draining. If you aren't living with purpose fueling you, it's pretty easy to get burnt out on the monotony of the day to day. What should be beautiful starts to feel mundane, and you can lose the meaning. That's one of the best things about purpose: it's burnout's kryptonite. When you are actively pursuing your purpose, it can help keep burnout at bay. Purpose opens the door and allows meaning to pour in. Just don't completely overextend yourself like I did. Keep tabs on the big picture. Too much of a good thing is still too much.

CHECK YOUR LEVELS

My dad always says when your gas tank is halfway empty, fill it up. He was always looking out for me because he knew I was the type of person who would push it and not fill up until my gas light had been on for an hour. He didn't want me to end up stranded on the side of the road. But come on, when the light goes on we all know we have at least ten more miles, right? Wrong. By the time the light goes on, your tank is already empty, and you are basically running on fumes. Who wants to live on fumes? Running on empty gives everyone, including you, the worst version of yourself.

Time to check your life levels in the categories of Faith, Marriage, Family, Wellness, Work, and Fun. Add any others that are important to you. Give yourself a score between one and five. Then, in any category that needs some work, list one thing you could do to fill this tank. You aren't going to be able to tackle every category at once, so decide which ones are the priority for you in this season of your life, and do one thing at a time. Checking in to this list as you go will serve as your gas light, reminding you to refuel.

 FAITH:

 MARRIAGE:

love what you do.

 FAMILY:

 WELLNESS:

 WORK:

 FUN:

ARE YOU OK? That one simple, but powerful question I was asked allowed me to change the direction of my life. It's OK to be overwhelmed or underwhelmed and not be OK. That's why we have each other. Reach out to someone on your Wise Council and share with them if you aren't OK. You'll both be glad you did.

If you are in a good place right now, look around and see if there is someone in your life who seems like they might be on the brink of burnout. Are you brave enough for a little positive disruption? Channel Lisa Dimson, take them out to lunch, and ask them if they are OK. It could change their life. I know it did mine!

"I had to come to terms

with the fact that I can do

anything, but I can't

do *everything*."

NINE

refuel.

So how do you keep from burning out and crashing hard? How do you stay inspired and on fire about what you're doing day after day, month after month, year after year? Because no matter how noble, meaningful, or inspiring the work we're doing is, if we are so stressed we can barely function, it will feel like a burden and push you right into burnout. You will start to resent it and eventually stall out or quit. It's just how it works, whether you are a mom going through the day to day of raising little ones or working a high-pressure corporate job. We all need to take care of our minds, bodies, and souls so that we stay fueled and have plenty to pour out to others. You can't pour from an empty pitcher.

First and foremost, if you want to stay fueled, you

must learn to rest. I was a little nervous when Lisa first suggested a sabbatical, because I thought I was going to have to lie in bed all day and do nothing, and that just isn't me. I have way too much energy for that! But sabbatical comes from the word "Sabbath." After God created our world, in Genesis 1:31, he rested and looked at his work and saw that "it was very good." But God didn't just take a well-deserved nap after making the entire world and everything in it; he used that seventh day as time to reflect on and appreciate the good work he had done. If all I did with my sabbatical was sleep, spend time with my family, and do some fun stuff, I may have felt better for a little while, but it wouldn't have been enough to keep burnout at bay. I needed to use my sabbatical like God used the Sabbath. I needed to look at my life from the outside with reflection, joy, and gratitude instead of just churning out work and moving on. The more I learned about the concept of Sabbath, the more I longed to find rest in God instead of just grasping blindly for temporary solutions. I didn't want temporary rest—I wanted true rest that energizes the soul.

I tend to go through about a six-year cycle of working myself to burnout before hitting the wall and being forced to rest, reset, and reinspire myself. I was about six years out of college when I left my corporate job to become an entrepreneur and start fab'rik. About six years after that, I hit a wall, lacking the purpose of my growing company, and found that renewed energy I was missing in Haiti. Six years after that, Angelo could see the burnout coming and swept me away for a surprise vacay to Harbour Island, Bahamas. I was so exhausted that I fainted our first night there and broke my jaw, knocking out most of my teeth. I spent months recuperating with my jaw wired shut, unable to talk or eat solid food. Let me tell you, there is nothing fashionable about a feeding tube. It was six years later that I ended up on sabbatical. Clearly, I needed to make some big changes if I didn't want to be back in the same burnt-out spot in another six years. Nothing in nature blooms all year round, and neither can we. I needed to figure out how to refuel regularly and how to take smaller breaks more often. I run a company with hundreds of women watching me, and I'd crashed and burned hard right in front of all of them. I loved every single person on my team so much, and in the process of burning out, I'd made them feel less than, not trusted, and not good enough for me. And that couldn't be further from the truth. I felt like I owed it to myself and to them to do this sabbatical thing right, to fix what I'd broken in myself and within my company. I wanted to learn why this happened and how to prevent it, then share that knowledge with them. I couldn't imagine anyone on my team having to go through this.

CLEAN IT OUT

I mean, you've been there, right? You might not have broken your jaw, but we've all had times where we've

lost that loving feeling—gone from heart eyes about
what you do to feeling totally blah about things that
used to light your soul on fire. There are a few things
that contribute to burnout. Usually you are either
working waaaaaayyyy too much, you aren't challenged enough, or you are doing too many things
and not doing any of them well anymore (or a combo
of all three!). Yikes! So if you are starting to feel like
you are sliding toward burnout, hit the pause button, jump off the hamster wheel, and reassess. Not
everyone needs a three-month sabbatical like me, and
frankly, not everyone can take that. I would simply
start with cleaning out your closet, literally and figura-
tively, which is exactly what I did on my very first day
of my sabbatical.

Cleaning out my closet is so therapeutic for me.
That morning, I turned on my dance party playlist
and hauled every single item out of my closet and
drawers. I was on a mission to get back to basics and
embrace a little minimalism. I'd made myself a list
of wardrobe basics, and I combed through my piles
of clothes in search of items on the list. If I had it
already, great; if not, I'd go shopping later to find the
perfect piece. I needed a flattering pair of dark jeans,
a casual pair of jeans, a pair of simple black heels,
a pair of black flats, a black leather jacket, a white
silky button down, a basic neutral clutch, a jean jacket
and a few other wardrobe must-haves. I needed to get
these basics right, because they are the foundation of
any versatile wardrobe.

Then I moved to decluttering. I didn't need ten gold layering necklaces or thirty pairs of distressed jeans. Yes, there is too much of a good thing! I tried everything on, and it was brutal. Anything that didn't make me feel beautiful went directly into my free fab'rik donation bin—and it was a *huge* pile by the end. Hint: This should be an easy yes or no, so if you hesitate, then it's a no. After all of that, I still had one pile of clothing left to tackle. These clothes weren't wardrobe staples, I couldn't think of anywhere I would wear them, and they weren't practical (think a long, white tulle skirt or sequin tee), but I smiled every time I looked at them. Some I had worn before and loved the memories they carried, but I was still searching for the right place to wear the rest. They were dream outfits that may never be worn, but they deserved a spot in my closet just because I loved them so much. They represented all of the happy things I'd been missing in my life for months. The wow, wacky, unproductive simply joyful things I really needed to find again. I had Angelo haul everything else off to free fab'rik since I wasn't allowed in the office, and I felt great knowing my clothes would be going to good homes soon.

Cleaning out my closet felt so incredibly cathartic, and I realized that it needed to be my blueprint for my sabbatical. I needed to yank everything out, declutter, try everything on with fresh eyes, and then only put the things that really belonged there back into my life—the basics like time with God, my family, and friends, and the things that fueled me, gave me joy, and brought the WOW. If I could clean out my closet, I could clean out my life, and I knew I'd be a lot better off for having done the work.

My next order of business was to clear out everything I could. I started with my calendar and cancelled all of my guilt plans, every coffee, every event, every lunch, every party, and every call. My schedule went from having twenty-five items each day to two. It felt liberating. Initially I had a lot of big plans for my sabbatical. I thought I'd take Asher back to Ethiopia to see where she was born or maybe even go to Cali and learn to surf. But the more I thought about it, the more the idea of simply living my life—my current, imperfect but totally blessed life—moved to the top of my list. So instead of booking plane tickets, I gave my nanny a sabbatical. I decided that I would go to bed at a normal hour and cook the eggs from our chickens with real bacon in the mornings for my kids. I would sit down with my family at dinner each night. I would do carpool and help with homework and maybe even have the energy to have a conversation with the love of my life when he walked in the door after a long day. I would get my small group back together and dive back into God's word. The more I thought about it, the more blissful it seemed. Turns out the ultimate luxury for me at that point was just being home. I needed the rest and routine, but even more than that, I needed the time to figure out the core of my own personal happiness.

BRING ON THE FUN!

If I had one day to do all the fun (completely unproductive!) things I wanted, what would I do? When I thought about what would make me happy, my mind would default to lying on the beach at a luxury villa in Bali, reading my favorite book with a glass of champagne. Of course that would make me happy— that would make anyone happy. But I knew I was just visualizing a basic, generic version of happiness instead of activities that were specific to me, which was pretty pathetic and tells you how far off course I had gotten as someone who has always had an oversized imagination. I'd gotten so far away from experiencing the little joys of everyday life that I was basically dreaming of the stock image that comes with a frame instead of filling the frame with my own incredible artwork. (Plus, you can't go to Bali every week. I needed fun stuff that I could do on the regular!) I had lost the play, the fun, the unscheduled joy in my life. The laughing until you cry phone calls with my sister, yoga with my friends, long walks with my pups, Cowboy and Vader, and dinners with my fab'rik team had fallen off the calendar months before, and I knew I was worse off for missing them. There was so much good in my life, so where had the happy gone? My working theory was that if I found that, it would fuel my soul, kick-start my inspiration engine, and I'd be back on track with passion and purpose. So I dove headfirst into finding it.

I called my sister, Erin, and we begged our husbands to pick up the kids from carpool that day and headed to a lake house about an hour away for the night. We called this trip our sister sabbatical. We packed almost nothing except books, bikinis, and snacks. We made lists of things that made us happy and goals for the next month. Erin, as my baby sister, was my very first best friend, and we know each other better than anyone else, so it's easy to be honest and completely myself with her. I came home with a sore belly from laughing, a list of goals, and an I-can-conquer-the-world attitude I'd been missing for a while. I needed that joy! Instead of opening my laptop every night after dinner, I poured two glasses of wine and pulled my husband out on the back porch so we could snuggle and talk about our days. Saturday nights became date nights, and we adventured into unfamiliar neighborhoods to try new restaurants and fun activities like we used to when we were first dating. The rough areas between us caused by too little time together and too much stress smoothed out, and I felt like a newlywed again, only better. Angelo got his wife back, and I gained a new appreciation for my patient husband.

Next, I decided to sign up for hip-hop classes. (Yes, I'm in my forties and am taking hip-hop classes. Follow your dreams.) I'd never taken dance classes, but I love to dance, so I thought, why not go for it? I was more nervous for the first class than I have ever been speaking on stage to thousands of people. I had this-is-crazy-but-I-can't-wait-to-start butterflies in my stomach. It took me about an hour to figure out what to wear, since the hip-hop dance section of my closet was nonexistent. Then I spent the drive over trying to come up with excuses to cancel. Luckily, I was on sabbatical, so I had no ready excuses and nowhere else to be.

I twisted my hair up into a sloppy bun and secured it with the hairband I'd been holding in my teeth. I checked my reflection one last time in my rearview mirror. I smiled at my reflection. For a moment there, I'd gotten a glimpse of the dreamer, adventurer, joyful Dana that I wanted to get back to so badly. I really missed her. I wasn't wearing any makeup, but I looked more alert and rested than I had in years. My sabbatical was definitely helping me get more sleep. I took a deep breath and then got out of my car and headed into the dance studio, thinking, *Please don't let me be the oldest person in the class.*

My sneakers squeaked a little on the light wood floors as I approached the front desk.

"Hey, I'm Dana," I said. "I'm here for the hip-hop class."

"Cool" the receptionist said warmly. "Are you a dancer?"

"If you count morning dance parties with my kids, then yes," I replied.

She laughed. "That totally counts. Is this your first time?"

"Yes, definitely."

"OK, well, fill out these papers, and we'll get you set up. You're going to love it."

"Do you get a lot of new dancers?" I asked while I scrawled my name, address, and emergency contact info on the form she'd provided and signed a waiver.

"Not a ton," she replied. I must have looked nervous. "But don't worry—I'm sure you'll pick it right up."

She sent me down the hall to the large dance studio. I stashed my bag and shoes in a cubby and walked into the room. Drake was blaring out of the speakers, and dancers were laughing and chatting while they stretched. The huge room was dimly lit with floor-to-ceiling mirrors on three walls. The last wall was glass, allowing people in the hallway to watch the class. Seriously? The idea of strangers watching me made me even more nervous. I sat down on the floor and pretended to stretch, too, but I wasn't really sure what I was supposed to be stretching. Everyone around me was so limber. (Two girls were actually carrying on a conversation while they were both doing the literal splits. Talk about intimidating!) The other dancers were all wearing baggy pants and leg warmers. Who knew leg warmers were back in style? I took mental notes so I would know exactly what to wear next time if I made it through this class.

"Hey," said the girl next to me. "Is this your first time? I don't think I've seen you before."

"Yep," I said, smiling nervously. "I have no idea what I'm doing, so I'll probably be a mess."

"Don't worry about getting it right, just have fun," she said as she shook her shoulders back and forth with the world's best rhythm.

Just have fun? It had been a long time since I had done something without a purpose, with a goal to just have fun. I loved that idea.

Just then the instructor came in. "What's up, everybody?" He asked as everyone clapped. He looked right at me. "For our new faces, this is how it goes: we learn an entire set and go through it a few times as a group, and then everyone performs in pairs. Are we ready to do this?" He clapped his hands, and someone changed the music.

Everyone stood up and spaced themselves out in loose lines. I stayed in the back-right corner and did my best to keep up. The instructor moved quickly, showing us moves while counting like a drill sergeant. "One, two, three, four, then five, six, seven, eight."

Once we started dancing, my nerves melted away. I focused so intently on the steps that I forgot to think about how I felt. I stopped caring what anyone else thought and started being present. Typically, I don't like to do things I'm not good at. Like ever. But today I was OK not being the best. Which—surprise, surprise—I wasn't. It was so freeing to be able to let go of any expectations and Just. Have. Fun.

At the end of the class, we performed the dance in pairs. My partner was incredible—she hit every move. I was less incredible, but had just as much fun. I was laughing so hard trying to catch up at the part where we flipped our heads around and threw our hands to our knees. I almost fell over, but it was everything I could have asked for. Unproductive, no rules, can't stop laughing and singing kind of fun. All of the other dancers were cheering me on. It was the first time in a long time that I felt like it was OK not to get it right, not to have to all the right answers, and mostly not to have to lead. I could just try to keep up, learn, and figure it out as I went. It made me feel carefree and alive in a way that I realized I hadn't in far longer than was OK.

After everyone finished up, I grabbed my stuff and walked next door to a juice bar. I ordered a detox drink, hopped in my car, rolled down the windows, and turned on LL Cool J's "Loungin'." I drove home with the windows down, wind whipping through my hair, the sun warm on my face, singing at the top of my lungs, just like I used to before I became a perpetually stressed out, overly busy grownup. I would definitely be going back for another class. Why had I let myself miss out on this feeling for so long? Why did it feel like I'd forgotten how to have fun? I have always loved hip-hop music, and my sister and I spent almost every afternoon making up dances in our living room and making our brother, Sean, watch us perform to Chaka Khan in middle school. But as we get older, stuff like that slips to the bottom and then falls off the list altogether when all of our time is spent on conference calls, making dinner, running errands, and trying to remember who needs new shoes and underwear at any given time. We're all doing ourselves such a disservice by not prioritizing the stuff that fills us up and makes us feel like we can conquer the world. Because when we're filled up, we have so much more to pour out to everyone who needs us.

Sometimes you just need to step away from everyone else and feed your soul. Use a PTO day, or just pick a random Saturday. Don't be productive—just have fun. Go out there and try something new you've always wanted to do. Build a garden, ride a horse, go to a museum, or simply do nothing. Sign up for a hip-hop class with me. You *need* this. Grab your favorite person, and get out of town for a mini sabbatical. You don't have to sightsee or spend a lot of money. Just hang out with the person who makes you laugh until you cry. Go on a date with your boyfriend or husband in the middle of the day. Do not talk about work or kids or logistics. Spending time together doing nothing but having fun is such a luxury. Read a new devotional, or just open your Bible and get lost in God's Word. Try to do this sort of stuff more often—every week or every month. Think you don't have time? I bet you can look through your calendar and find a few plans you've said yes to out of guilt. Cancel them. Your time is precious, and you have too many amazing things to accomplish to spend any of it on unnecessary stuff that you really don't want to do. Clearing your calendar can give you a fresh perspective you've been lacking. Go back to basics for a while, and see what you miss and what you can't wait to add back in.

Those are the things that are going to keep you fueled and combat burnout. If you don't miss it, let go of the guilt, and don't let it sneak back onto your to-do list.

BUILD IN BOUNDARIES

I wish I could say that I got home from hip-hop class a new woman and that all my problems were solved by the power of dance, but life is a lot more complicated than that. What did happen is that I felt really inspired by finding ways to infuse my life with fun again. I wanted to build those things into my routine and schedule to make sure they didn't fall off of my to-do list when I went back to work. I knew that on my first day back at fab'rik, I would be faced with a flood of meeting requests, e-mails, and phone calls that would feel totally overwhelming. I needed guardrails. I needed to intentionally set up boundaries and a framework that allowed me time for passion, purpose, dreaming, and fun.

The real keys, for me, would have to be my calendar and my to-do list. They controlled my time, so they needed to be where my guardrails lived. You can tell a lot about anyone's heart by looking at how they spend their time. I needed to intentionally align my time and my heart. For the life that I wanted, I had to build in margin and learn to say no. Nothing ever goes exactly according to plan, so now I've learned to plan for that. Instead of trying to squeeze in every little meeting, conversation, and invitation, and feeling like I couldn't cancel a thing, I map out my week every Sunday. I put down the things that are nonnegotiable—the commitments that only I can do—in one color and the things that are negotiable in another. Those things that must happen, those are heart things that I have committed to, like taking my kids to school, going to Hudson's football game to cheer for him, attending doctors' appointments and speaking engagements, having quiet time with God each morning, and going on date nights with Angelo. It felt weird at first, this new militant devotion to putting my time where my heart is, but I got used to it fast because it made life so much better. Things like doctors' appointments and date nights used to get cancelled, but now they are essentially written in stone. And I added back in time with God as nonnegotiable. Instead of falling asleep praying, I started my days clear-eyed and open-hearted with him. A friend suggested I read the book of Philippians each morning for thirty days. I was hooked after a week. I couldn't believe how much richer and deeper those words became to me with each passing day.

Of course, this means I've had to get good at saying no. If you want to do big things and make big dreams happen, you have to prioritize the things that will get you to where you want to be, including doing things that keep you fueled and inspired. This is where it's OK to look at your life and say, "You know what, I'm no longer going to try to be that." For me it looks like accepting the fact that I'm not going to be the mom who bakes homemade brownies for the bake sale or class parties. I'm just not. I'd rather pick some up from the bakery so I have time to make it to a free fab'rik spree or watch a movie with my kids before they go to bed. I've cut "Pinterest-worthy baker" from the list of "who I thought I should be and what I thought I should be doing." (There's that bad word *should* again!) I don't let myself feel guilty about it anymore. Letting go of who I felt I should be means I have the time and space to do things I want to do so I can be the person I want to be. My kids need a happy mommy to laugh with them, not a frazzled, flour-covered mom yelling about burnt brownies because I was trying to multitask.

So when should you say yes, and when should you say no? It's going to be different for everyone, but I set some ground rules for myself that have really helped. I want to say yes to everything. Saying yes is fun and exciting and it makes people happy. I love making people happy. Which is exactly why I have these guidelines to help me. Every time I get a request to do something, speak somewhere, or sign up for a board or committee, I scroll through a few questions in my head to help me figure out my best answer. Is this something only I can do? Then I say yes. A "Tea with Mom" event at Asher's school: yes, that's me! No one else can be my child's mom. At work, no one else can give a speech casting the vision for the company. I'm the only founder of fab'rik, so that one's mine! Is this something that I would look forward to all week or all year? Heck yeah, I'm saying yes! Is the person asking someone who matters deeply to me, and does what they are asking for matter deeply to them? That's a "Heck, yes!" too. Is this something that is good for me and my health? I have learned to say yes to things that keep me healthy and whole as much as I can, like regular sessions with my counselor or yoga with my friend, Andrea. Does this opportunity align with my purpose? If not, it's a no, no matter how great of a cause it is. I've found my purpose, and I need to stay in my lane. Just because I *can* doesn't mean I *should*. Of course, sometimes you have to say yes to stuff that doesn't fit the criteria, because that's just life. But having these guidelines helps me choose my yeses more intentionally and helps keep from wasting my most valuable resource: time.

I told you already that I'm famous at work for saying "there's a yes in every no," which sounds confusing until you really think about it. Every time you say no to something that's not where you should be, you've given yourself the gift of being able to say yes to something that is. Basically, every no is just a different yes waiting to happen. And that's true, too, when someone says no to you or when you feel like the world is telling you no over and over. If someone tells you no, they've given you the gift of not wasting your time on the wrong person or wrong mission. When the world says no, it's just redirecting you. So take that no, say thank you, and keep marching forward, looking for your yes.

BE PRESENT

You might be thinking to yourself, "In the last chapter you were a mess. Your team basically begged you to take a sabbatical, so why should I listen to anything you have to say about how to stay fueled?" Well, you'd be right. I did burn out. Big time. I didn't know a thing about rest or refueling then, but I've learned a lot. I've done a lot of work to figure out why I burn out and how I could keep it from happening again. And I'm not talking about work-life balance. I don't pretend to have balance figured out. The idea that you should go to bed every night at 9:00 p.m. and go to the gym every day and leave work at 5:00 p.m. on the dot is nice. But it doesn't work for most of us. If you've found the secret, please share it with the rest of us!

Here's the thing: I've honestly never met anyone balanced who was busy changing the world. Which is why, for me, it's not about balance as much as it is about presence. You have to prioritize where you are when you're there, both physically and emotionally, so you can be there for the people who need you. I used to think multitasking was the best thing in the world—I can be at the playground and handle a conference call from work! No, I can't. I tried that for years, and the second it was time for my call, my son would fall and scrape his knee, I'd mute my call to ask other parents for a Band-Aid, quietly console him, and finally un-mute, having no idea what we were talking about. No one got my very best in those scenarios, and I felt like I was letting everyone down.

So now, when I'm at work, I'm all in at work. I'm not thinking about my home to-do list, the "All About Me" project I need to do with Ryder when I get home, Lincoln's upcoming birthday party plans, date night with my husband (OK, so I do daydream about that for a minute or two a day—I'm only human!), or errands I need to run. I'm thinking about how I can create a free fab'rik fundraising plan with Kayla. She has my time, my attention, and my heart. And when I'm at home, I try to turn work off. When we are having our morning dance parties to Wham! songs, I'm not mentally prepping for my strategic planning meeting with my executive coach. And when I'm on date night with Angelo, I'm *definitely* not thinking about fourth quarter initiatives or laundry. I now strive to be as present in each moment as I possibly can so that I'm getting the most out of that time and giving the best of me to whoever I'm with. My work is better when I do this, and I'm a better mom, wife, and friend when I'm present with the people I love. It takes some work and discipline (my phone has a box it lives in from 5:00 to 7:00 p.m., just in case I get tempted!), but it's so worth it.

WHAT GOT YOU HERE WON'T GET YOU THERE

My sabbatical was all about cleaning out the clutter in my closet, my schedule, and my soul and then refilling my life with the things I really need for the season I'm in. As you grow, what feeds your soul changes, so what is on your schedule should, too. It was about saying no to the stuff I didn't need so I could say yes to the stuff I did. One of the things I added back to my calendar was meetings with my counselor. In our first meeting, I asked point blank if I was going through a breakdown. She smiled and told me that breakdowns and breakthroughs are very similar. (So, basically, yes.) When you're going through a breakdown, you're deconstructing the pieces of yourself that you no longer need. It means you're growing and evolving into who you need to be for the next phase of your life. You have to let go of the things and parts of yourself that are holding you back to make room for the new parts of your personality to grow and flourish in the next chapters of your life. I wanted my sabbatical to be a breakthrough, which meant I needed to get through the breakdown first. That looks like putting all the pieces of yourself on the table, examining them, and accepting that you're going to need to be rebuilt for who you are becoming. You'll have to let go of some of the pieces of yourself that brought you to where you are today and be OK with picking up new skills that will take you even further.

Going on a silent retreat was one of the most powerful things I did on my sabbatical. I know, I know, who wants to go to a place where you can't talk for four days? *Me!* I had been the face and voice of fab'rik for so long that the idea of going days without answering someone's question, solving a problem, or weighing in on something sounded exactly like what I needed. The retreat was the most dramatic thing I did during this sabbatical. When your days are jammed full of back-to-back meetings, conference calls at all hours, trying to fit in family and time with kids, and then working until late into the night, you can't even hear your own inner voice, let alone God's. So I took four days and checked out of life and into the monastery.

My best friend thought I may be losing it. Why would I pick not talking at a silent retreat over a beach vacation with her if I needed a getaway? I wasn't entirely sure myself, but I knew I was craving alone time and peace and quiet. The first day was a little weird, and I had to really stop myself from talking, even if only to myself in my room. I hadn't realized how often I used catching up on phone calls or making small talk as a way to escape from my own thoughts. But without those distractions, I had nothing to do except confront all of the thoughts roaming around my head. I spent the next four days fasting, reading, journaling, going for jogs, doing yoga, and praying. I was hungry and tired (each day started with 4:00 a.m. prayer time), but it was a such a powerful way for me to dig deep into what I really needed. I realized on that retreat that I just may be an introvert. Who knew? I love being around people, but I need time alone to refuel and recharge. I hadn't been alone with just myself for more than an hour or two since my oldest was born. No wonder I was struggling so much!

I think what was really so impactful for me was that I didn't spend most of the time thinking about fab'rik or my family or my friends or orphans or sex trafficking—at least not after that first day. I spent the time thinking about myself. I thought about what made me happy. Only this time I wasn't thinking about big stuff like passion or purpose—I was just thinking about small things in life. Going to church feeds my soul. Going on family vacations really makes me happy. Long runs are my favorite way to spend an extra hour. Eating meals together as a family centers me. Making it to my best friends' birthday dinners and girls' nights brings me tons of joy. Sitting with my stylists and hearing what they love about fab'rik inspires me, but I wasn't making any of that a priority. I left the retreat beyond ready for a massive bowl of Jinya's vegan spicy noodles, but feeling refreshed in a way I didn't know was possible. I'm doing it again this year because nothing in my life has calmed my thoughts and refreshed my soul so much.

My goal now is to keep myself fueled, inspired, and growing. I feel like I've figured out where I tend to go off track and asked my Wise Council to help keep me on the rails. After going back to basics for my sabbatical, I slowly started to add back in the things I wanted to be doing and the things I need to do to stay healthy. I didn't rehire my nanny. Instead, I go into the office later and leave earlier so I can take my kids to school and pick them up. It's my favorite part of each day because it gives me a chance for great conversations with them and it keeps me in tune with their school lives. I kept date nights with my husband, family dinners with my parents, and girls' nights with my best friends. I kept hip-hop classes and counseling sessions and church every Sunday. I now get six or more hours of sleep every night, drink plenty of water, and keep up with maintenance like going to the doctor and dentist and taking my car into the shop as soon as that check engine light blinks on. I clean out my closet, my inbox, and my calendar regularly. I re-organize and unsubscribe from e-mails, social media accounts, and anything else that makes me feel like I'm not doing enough. I try new foods, new exercises, and new parts of town, and I go outside of my comfort zone whenever I can to keep a sense of adventure and exploration alive in my heart. And I haven't run out of gas once since my sabbatical. I do small gut checks often to make sure the things I'm doing are keeping me fueled and inspired so that I have plenty to give to the people in my life that really matter. And I do all of it with plenty of dance parties!

REFUEL

Cleaning out my closet was the blueprint for my sabbatical. I needed to yank everything out, declutter, try everything on with fresh eyes, and then only put the things that really belonged there back into my life—the basics like my family, friends, and faith, and the things that fueled me and brought the happy WOW.

If I could clean out my closet, I could clean out my life, and I knew I'd be a lot better off for having done the work.

Now, it's your turn. Imagine pulling everything out of your life's closet, drawers, and storage. Now what will you add back in?

? BASICS: What foundational pieces are missing? What needs to be fixed—an obvious area you have been ignoring?

? DECLUTTER: What do you have too much of? What's an area you need to clear out to give you some much-needed margin?

? EXPLORE: What makes you feel like yourself? What challenges and excites you? What makes you happy? What is your version of my hip-hop dance class?

? BUILD IN: What needs to be prioritized or cancelled on your calendar? What are the things in your schedule that only you can do?

💬 WISE COUNCIL TEXT: I need to plan a night of fun. What should we do?

"It's not about balance

as much as it is

about presence."

TEN

chief visionary officer.

At exactly 10:00 a.m. my phone rang with fab'rik's Chief Marketing Officer and current acting CEO's ringtone.

"Lisa!" I answered. A cool breeze that felt like fall ruffled my hair, and I snuggled more deeply into my cozy sweater. I was sitting on my back porch enjoying my morning fab'rik latte.

"Dana!" she exclaimed. It was really good to hear her voice. She sounded energetic, and I could hear the murmur of my fab'rik family working in the background—the familiar sounds of the office on a Wednesday morning. A small wave of homesickness washed through me. fab'rik had been as much home to me as my actual house for the past fifteen years. I didn't realize that hearing that bustle would make me miss it so much. "How are you? We all miss you!"

"I'm really good and miss y'all more," I said, and I meant it wholeheartedly. That little twinge of home-sickness for the office aside, I was doing really well. I stood up and began pacing around the backyard, walking between the pool and the bocce ball court along a well-worn path. While neither Lisa nor I had a plan for what the outcome of my sabbatical would be, we both hoped and prayed it would give me vision for what was next for me and fab'rik. My time away had offered just that. My head was clear, and my heart was wide open. I felt like myself again. I shared a little about what I had been up to, and she shared a little of what she was up to, but there was really only one thing I wanted to know. I looked down at my feet and watched the fluffy back pom-poms on the ends of my snowflake slippers bouncing with each step I took. "So . . ." I sat down on the grass and laid back to brace myself. "How are things at fab'rik?" I finally asked and closed my eyes.

There were only two possible answers to this question, and while I had played them both over and over in my head before the call, I still wasn't entirely sure which one I was hoping for. If Lisa told me that the company was struggling, they all missed me like crazy, and were lost without me, I would know that fab'rik couldn't stand on its own two feet and that, without my relentless pouring into it, it would fail. I would have to jump back in full force to the day to day of my business and figure out how to live with the weight of the world on my shoulders. What other choice would I have? But if Lisa told me that fab'rik was better than ever, that they didn't need me, I would probably feel hurt and lost and, frankly, like I'd been fired from my own dream. I closed my eyes and tried to ignore my swirling emotions so I could listen to Lisa's answer.

"Yeah, no, things are good," Lisa said.

"OK, tell me more," I replied cheerfully, trying to give her the go-ahead to be honest.

"Things are actually really good," she admitted, and I could hear pride in her voice. "The team has stepped up in a huge way. Kayla is killing it with free fab'rik. We're up to three free sprees a week. Ally's team has streamlined a lot of the inventory process issues, and our margins are in such a great place. Our new marketing campaigns are in full effect, and the store managers are really excited. You're really going to be so happy when you get back. Everyone is so confident in their roles, making great decisions, taking on leadership. Dana, you would be so proud."

I exhaled in relief as Lisa continued. I loved what I was hearing. Then I felt relieved to be relieved! She was right—I was proud. They had it. I had been working myself up so much in anticipation of that moment, and now that it was here, it just wasn't a big deal. "Thank you, Lisa, I don't think there could have been a better answer," I told her, beaming into my coffee cup.

"So, when are you coming back?" Lisa asked.

"Do you still want me back?" I asked. This was the

million-dollar question. "I don't want to come in and undo the progress you guys have made."

"Of course we want you back! Dana, the day to day of the business is thriving, but we need you for the big picture. I know you are the person that will dream bigger for us, challenge us, and inspire us. We need your vision," Lisa said frankly.

My team had fab'rik. I didn't have to take it all back on, but they still needed me. It was the best thing I could have heard.

"Well, I can't think of a single place I would rather be than actually focusing on our vision," I said.

"You can certainly jump back into meetings here at the corporate office and spend your time in spreadsheets and reports, but can you imagine what you could accomplish if you got to spend more time on what's next instead of what you have already created?" Lisa asked. I know, I know, I know, don't you totally want a Lisa in your life? Cheering you on and believing in you, even when you're broken?

"I actually can," I nodded emphatically, my entire soul already shifting to my new dream job.

"You created fab'rik. As the founder and CEO, you get to choose what your role is and what you think is best for your company and for yourself." Could it be that what was best for my company at this next juncture would be best for me too? "We need you, Dana," Lisa continued. "You are the face and heart of fab'rik. But we need you outside of this office sharing our vision, inspiring our teams to live it and our communities to feel it. We need our refueled, rested, and ready-to-go leader back igniting our purpose."

"I have no idea what it looks like yet, but I'm all in," I said. I felt that feeling that I thought I'd lost a year or so ago. I felt like myself, my bossy, big hearted, dreamer self about to take on my next dream job. I was ready for the next step. As CEO, I had been so entrenched in my comfort zone that I lost sight of my bold, fearless self. I was doing stuff that other people could easily do instead of being brave enough to step into the things that only I could do and was made to do. Things that really needed to be done, like sharing our fab'rik story through speaking engagements and growing our brand through WOW, over-the-top marketing and PR campaigns. Lisa was right. fab'rik couldn't grow unless I did. And I was beyond ready. "When do I start?"

I went back to work post-sabbatical with a renewed sense of passion, purpose, and vision. What I'd realized was that everything I'd built with fab'rik, from the stores to our e-commerce site to free fab'rik and Asher to annual mission trips and WOW experiences, all came from my vision. Yes, it took hard work from my team, and sacrifice, and prayer, and untold gallons of coffee, but none of that would have amounted to anything without my vision of everything I knew fab'rik could and can be. I could continue to try to do every job at fab'rik, but I didn't want to, and more importantly, I'd hired incredibly talented, capable, strong people that could do those jobs better than

I could! My job as the founder of fab'rik needed to be the vision caster. For us to grow and flourish and make the big impact I'd always dreamed of making, I needed to be charting our course and steering the ship and trusting my team to handle the mechanics of getting us there. I wanted to be challenging them to trust themselves and produce their best, most creative work. But I had to lead the way.

A big part of why I had been feeling so burnt out and stuck was that I had outgrown the CEO role and was really ready for the next step, but I wasn't courageous enough to just take it. And that's on me. Remember in chapter 7 when I asked you to draw a heart with two bigger hearts around it and to find your third heart? Well I was ready to draw my fourth heart. I was ready to grow fab'rik's heart, and my own, to accomplish even bigger things, but I had let fear of losing control of what I'd already built hold me back. I'd given my captain's hat to fear, and fear is a terrible navigator. My sabbatical gave me the time and space to see this, shake it off, and start dreaming about what would fill that next heart for fab'rik and for my life.

I decided my title would be CVO: Chief Visionary Officer. Something about replacing the word "executive" with "visionary" felt so much more me. We had never had a CVO, so I would have to create my own job description. In order to do that, I had to define what vision actually was and why we needed this role. Vision is really thinking about and planning the future with imagination, intention, and wisdom. Vision is basically the North Star we all need to navigate to our destination. So I needed to be able to imagine where our company could be and paint a picture of what that looked like for my team. It was no small feat, but it was second nature to me—I'd been doing that all along anyway. I was up for the task, but I couldn't be the CVO and the CEO at the same time without rushing right back to that burnout point, and no one wanted that.

Once upon a time, I would have thought that walking away from the CEO role meant I was quitting, and I don't quit. But I was actually growing. My company needed a CEO with fresh energy for the day to day to give our team new inspiration, and I needed a new challenge and the opportunity to focus my time where my heart was. Realizing something isn't working and having the courage to make big changes to fix it is the positive disruption Lisa had promised me when we'd gotten coffee all those months before. As the CVO, I get to be the face of fab'rik, speak to people around the nation about high style with heart and about the power of what happens when what you love intersects with what the world needs, and God-willing create an army of women who believe in dreaming big and serving bigger. I love that my new job entails keeping our company's heart beating so hard that we never lose sight of it. I had lost sight of what I loved and what I was meant to do, but by taking a break, getting really vulnerable, and never giving up on dreaming, I was able to create a new role for myself that keeps my heart beating so hard that I don't think I'll ever lose sight of what I love again.

Of course, that's all easier said than done. I hired an executive coach who has been a godsend. He helped us navigate through this transition because, let's face it, letting go can be tough, even when you're ready and willing. He helped Lisa, Ally, and me figure out what I would need to feel comfortable stepping into new roles and how we could keep me from falling back on old patterns of parachuting in because I felt out of control. This is why it's so important to know yourself, your superpowers, and, most important-ly, your blind spots. I had already let my team down once, and I couldn't imagine doing that ever again. I wanted my transition to CVO to be a success, so I knew I'd need a little help curbing my control freak behavior. I'm just thankful my team was so incredibly patient with me. Detoxing from my CEO role was ten thousand times harder than I expected—I want to be really honest about that. One day Ally changed the return policy, and you would have thought she'd cut my arm off. After a major, totally unjustified freak-out, I pulled myself back together and apologized. It was a return policy—no big deal—so why did I lose it? It wasn't because I didn't trust her to make the right decision. I totally trusted her with everything! It was that fab'rik was my first baby, and the thought of fully handing its day-to-day care to someone else went against every instinct I'd developed over the last sixteen years. I felt like I was giving fab'rik up for adoption. I knew it was what was best for my baby, but it still felt so difficult. I was explaining all this to one of my best friends when she told me she thought I needed to see it from a different perspective. She pointed out that fab'rik is sixteen years old. I've raised this baby into a functioning, wonderful adult who I'm essentially sending off to college or to start its own career. I will always be there, supporting and guiding, but my baby is a grownup who needs space to keep growing. That this is what my wish has been all along: for fab'rik to be able to thrive on its own. She was right, a different perspective changed everything. I wasn't abandoning fab'rik, I was letting it fly.

I formally became fab'rik's CVO in September 2018, a little over one year after my post-sabbatical return to fab'rik. As the CVO, my job is to dream big for what's next for our company and to share the fab'rik story on as many stages as I can. I get to help others craft their own missions and encourage them to live in the sweet spot where passion and purpose intersect every day, and it's a role I feel so very blessed to have for my own. Crafting the vision for fab'rik has always been my responsibility, but I can't tell you how luxurious it feels to be able to laser focus all of my time and energy on this oh-so-important task to lift our team and future to new heights. I now have time to seek out new inspiration, look into exciting opportunities for fab'rik, visit stores and spend time with my teams, and meet with leaders I admire who encourage me to go beyond what I ever thought was possible for my company. I've realized that my team works best when I am outside of the details and shooting for the moon. They don't need me to tell them how to do their jobs—they need me to celebrate them. They don't need to have exact directions—they just need a clear guiding light.

Embracing my role as CVO of fab'rik has really reminded me that I need to be the CVO of my own life too. And so do you! I can't get so lost in the details of homework, after-school activities, expenses, and grocery runs that I forget to dream big for my family and for myself. I want my life to teach my kids how to find their own passions and purposes and how to live and lead with vision and heart. That's a big responsibility, and going back to that vision over and over helps me check in and see how I'm doing as a parent.

I also know that my kids won't be little forever (I'm not crying—you're crying!), which means I need to have a bigger vision for myself outside of my role as a mom. fab'rik is obviously a big part of that, but I know that there is more out there in the world for me. I want to be out on the front lines of my purpose, grabbing girls' hands and helping rescue them from the darkness of sex trafficking. I want to help orphaned babies in Africa find families and actually be there when they finally meet. I want to share my story of passion and purpose and vision with every woman out there, because I hope to inspire you all to create a life on fire for yourself, not only because of what it will do for you, but because of what I know it will do for our world. I want to leave a legacy behind that my kids will proudly point to and say, "That's my mom!" with full hearts. I want to be intentional about finding the experiences and opportunities that continue to challenge me to grow and expand my heart even further. I'm building my fourth heart now. But what will the sixth heart look like? Or the tenth? I know it's up to me to figure that out and move toward that with purpose.

My vision for my company is to make women feel beautiful, one piece of fab'rik at a time. My vision for my life is to help women who have stopped dreaming learn how to dream again. I know I won't be able to create dreamers out of every one of the 3.7 billion women in our world, but maybe I can light a spark and ignite as many as I can to carry it on. This is why I'm writing this book. This is why I pour myself into fab'rik. This is why we have free fab'rik and Asher. This is why I adopted. This is my life's work, and I pray it will be part of my legacy, that I cared deeply for all of these women. Legacy isn't only for hundred-year-olds who have bridges dedicated to them—it's for regular people like us who believe we are here for a reason and we are going to find out why. What's yours?

CAST YOUR VISION

Vision and dreaming and intention and prayer are all closely intertwined for me. And if you really think about it, they likely are for you, too. Vision crafts what life will look like, dreaming gives hope to possibility, intention helps to create plans, and prayer gives it all over to God to make it bigger and better than it could ever be without him. You likely already have at least a loose vision for your life. Take the time to think about it and firm it up. It's pretty similar to dreaming, but to cast a clear vision, you have to start at the end instead of the beginning. If you were to write the story of your life, how would it end? What impact would you want your life to have had on others? Who did you inspire along the way? When you are lost, remember God's directing your steps, so there's no need to give in and let fear guide you. As you discover your passion and purpose, your vision will naturally become clearer and more focused. Check back in on this vision often. Are you on the right track? Have you gotten off course? If so, has that changed your course enough that it's time to reevaluate your vision? Or are you working your way back to where you want to be? How could you move ahead faster? Don't just drift and assume you'll magically make it to where you want to go. Because that just isn't going to happen.

At the end of the day, God made you to be exactly who you are, and you are doing great work by seeking his purpose for your life. You can't control everything, but you can plot your course. You get to choose to follow your passion, which opportunities you pursue, the advice you take, the purpose you fight for, and the relationships you cultivate. You are steering your own ship toward good, so don't get too frustrated when you run aground occasionally or let a tide take you off track. You are going to hit rough waters and weather your way through storms you never saw coming, but stay the course, hold tight to your vision, and believe everything is possible. So what's your vision for your life?

My hope for you is that you will take the first big, bold steps I've outlined in this book to love what you do. Remember, of course, that what you do isn't just your job—it isn't only being a mom or a manager—it is what you do with your life and why you do it. I want your life to be charged with passion so that the work you do feels like a privilege instead of something to get through every day. I want you to discover your purpose so that you feel like you are living life in high definition, that everything is clear and that everything matters. I want you to live in the sweet spot where your passion and purpose intersect, inspiring everyone around you with the peace and fire you've found that drives you. I want you to have a life full overflowing with good, meaningful work, but also one full of happiness and joy. My vision for you is a life you love that fuels you to pour out love to everyone around you. I hope you have the same vision for yourself. It's entirely up to you—go get it!

CHIEF VISIONARY OFFICER

Vision is all about the future. It's about what you see as possible for your life, and it's about painting a picture for yourself so clearly that you can almost already feel it happening. So let's start at the ending and work backward. What impact do you want to leave on this world? What do you want your spouse, your kids, and those you lived life with to say about you? Feel about you? If you were watching a movie of your life, which parts would you be so proud of? How can you build more of that into your day to day? Start there, and then work your way backward to create a life that you are proud to live, one that serves others and honors God.

 What are three adjectives you hope people would use to describe you and the life you lived? List each of those adjectives below, then try to write a few sentences to describe how you could create a life around each of those words.

-

-

-

 WISE COUNCIL TEXT: What three words would you use to describe me?

"I want your life to

be charged with passion

so that the work you do

feels like a privilege instead

of something to get

through every day."

acknowledgments.

Thank you to my incredible family who has stood by me and cheered me on through the rollercoaster that is this beautiful life. My sister Erin for being my BFF and for reading this entire book on her phone in two hours and giving me the most loving feedback imaginable.

A huge what-would-I-do-without-you to my friends who have made sure I play as hard as I work and who have given me a Bad Moms text group that keeps me updated on all of the school stuff I miss when I'm at work.

To my fab'rik customers, thank you to each and every single one of you. I absolutely know I would not be able to do a day of this without you supporting our mission and wearing our clothing!

My fab'rik family, new and old, who helped build

this company when it was just a dream and who support this dream today. So much goes on behind the scenes and I appreciate all the long hours and all of your big hearts. Lisa, I'll never forget our JCT lunch and you breathing new life into me and fab'rik. Thank you, Ally Melson, fab'rik's COO and my most loyal partner. I can't imagine doing this without you and frankly couldn't have.

To my Wise Council, thank you for answering my calls and texts and emails time after time, praying with me through broken times, drinking champagne with me through amazing times, telling me no, and telling me that you are never giving up on me.

Thank you to my Haiti Ladies for igniting my faith. Thank you, London, for introducing me to your mom, Shelley Giglio, and for introducing me to Emily Vogeltanz and the entire Passion City Church family who has grown my faith and love for Jesus more than I knew was imaginable.

To all of our free fab'rik partner organizations and Project 82 that trust us to come into your spaces and love on your people—thank you for demonstrating the hands and feet of God. Thank you, Jeff Shinabarger, for agreeing to be my mentor and teaching me the power of a story. Jeff Henderson, thank you for encouraging me to put these words in this book. Thank you, God, for writing this story, the highs and the lows, I'm grateful for every bit.

Angelo Spinola, thank you for being up for any and every adventure our life has given us and being by my side through it all.

Lastly, to my sweet and strong Hudson, my giggling and loving Lincoln, world's best hugger Ryder, and little Wonder Woman Asher . . . you four kids are the light of my life. Thank you for the grace you've shown your mommy.